**Infinitely Determinable**

Davide Giuriato

**Infinitely Determinable**
**Children and Childhood in Modern Literature**

**Translated from the German**
**by Paul Bowman**

**DIAPHANES**

**THINK ART** Series of the Institute for Critical Theory (ith)—
Zurich University of the Arts and the Centre for Arts and
Cultural Theory (ZKK)—University of Zurich.

ISBN 978-3-0358-0316-7

Layout: 2edit, Zurich
Printed in Germany

www.diaphanes.com

# Table of Contents

*For Cecilia, my mother*

# Introduction

## I.

One of the still hardly disputed premises of recent research into childhood is the assumption that its very subject matter, childhood itself, is not to be analyzed as something natural but as a cultural phenomenon, one that, possessing its own history, has a beginning and possibly even an end.[1] As the historian of mentalities Philippe Ariès showed in his path-breaking 1960 study *L'Enfant et la vie familiale sous l'Ancien Régime*, "childhood" is not to be understood as an anthropological universal but as a cultural idea that, at a specific juncture in the history of Western societies, arose and proceeded to determine social discourse.[2] On the back of this assumption, the "discovery of childhood" soon launched its career: according to Ariès, what we have become used to calling "childhood" was not always already given—it is rather the continuation of an invention that goes hand in hand with the formation of the bourgeois subject and the nuclear family in the Early Modern period and then more specifically in the eighteenth century, before becoming the prevalent reality around and after 1800. The spreading of bourgeois culture in the Modern Age is, accordingly, to be considered the *historical a priori* of an idea of "childhood" that has remained dominant to the present day.

Although Ariès was frequently criticized for neglecting childhood in Antiquity and the Middle Ages, it remains incontestable that childhood, formerly only of isolated interest, begins to attract increasing attention in the seventeenth and eighteenth centuries, and crucially this attention is qualitatively different to the norms of premodern practices and customs.[3] Whereas traditional societies as a rule perceive the child merely as a small grownup, to whom no special emotional relationship needs to be maintained, the Modern Age proceeds from a categorical difference between children and adults.[4] This pertains to *structures* both internal and external to the family. Firstly, as part of a set of socio-cultural shifts of epochal significance, the child is moved to the middle of the family organization. Unlike traditional societies, the bourgeois nuclear family is organized around the newborn as its emotional center, and all affective energies are drawn to it, and so much so that for broad sections of society the newborn becomes the paramount reason for family life.[5] Secondly, this heightened concern for the welfare of the child is tangible everywhere outside the home as well. Not only does it gradually determine new discussions and attitudes in legal, pedagogic, scientific, economic, or demographic discourses,[6] the concept of "childhood" itself also changes, in so far as for the very first time it is conceived in terms of a space of shelter and protection that, for the purposes of upbringing and education, essentially serves to seal off the child from the harshness of adult life. The more it is conceived of as a form of existence that demands special and constant attention, then the more distinctively it needs to be separated from the adult domain.

The heightened concern for the welfare of the child thus has had a reverse side since the Modern Age: above all else due to the general instalment of a school system, a distinctive differentiation of spheres occurs in public space. The modern discovery of childhood constitutes, "in comparison to the integrative social forms of the Middle Ages, a growing dissociation between adults and children"[7] that finds expression in an ongoing isolating of the offspring and, at least ostensibly, an independent reality of their living environments. The

Swiss sociologist Franz-Xaver Kaufmann has described this as a "cloistering away from society"—in Modernity, according to Kaufmann, children are "structurally excluded from all major areas of life."[8] As described by Ariès, the "discovery of childhood" thus bears the imprint of an ambivalence characteristic of care and concern: the emotional affection for those growing up is entwined with an increasing distance towards them, installing a relationship of intimate closeness while maintaining great distance.

To the same degree that modern societies embrace their offspring to usher all of them, through education, into the domain of culture and order, the child evokes epistemic efforts to trace the unknown peculiarities of the infant mode of existence. In the eighteenth century, an interest in the child as entity *sui generis* is awoken in highly diverse contexts. While pedagogy leads the way, an understanding of "childhood" also comes to prominence in empirical psychology and anthropology that corresponds to the new social status of the offspring: the child is no longer seen as a "small adult" but rather as a "not-yet-grownup being." Similarly, the idea of an alterity figure is established, one that follows its own inherent logic and is distinguished by its own essentially intrinsic mode of thinking, perceiving, and acting. In the Modern Age, the child is the *Other* of the adult, defying fixation with rational concepts. Universally, it is addressed as a being that is *per definitionem* opposed to the adult:

> We know nothing of childhood; and with our mistaken notions the further we advance the further we go astray. [...] Childhood has its own ways of seeing, thinking, and feeling; nothing is more foolish than to try and substitute our ways.[9]

These much-quoted words from Jean-Jacques Rousseau's *Emile, or On Education*, the founding manifesto of modern pedagogy from 1762, are of exemplary significance for the relationship between the generations as it begins to configure in the bourgeois age. With succinct clarity, Rousseau encapsulates the premises underpinning the modern focus on the child. Without the slightest hint of idealization, it may be described as the "construct of an observer"[10] that, in the system of education, comes about through an unequivocal but not self-evident distinction of oppositions: in stark contrast to the adults, Rousseau paints the picture of a phase of life so removed from the adult world that there is a lack of any kind of notion for its inherent logic in every respect, and that, in its openness, needs to be protected from false or misguided demands and intrusive coopting. Drawing on Niklas Luhmann's clear-sighted consideration, it seems that the child is like a "black box," essentially "unknowable and uncontrollable," a source of "permanent irritating confusion."[11] Or in other words: with the "discovery of childhood," bourgeois culture delineates an arcane realm that, scarcely accessible to adults, serves as a projection space for ascriptions which are not only crassly contradictory but also bear the imprint of diverging ideologies. Whenever since the eighteenth century the child, as a baffling creature, becomes the focus of increasing attention, it appears as an alien being unceasingly evoking uncertainty and insecurity, although, concurrently, it is exposed to perpetual territorialization—because the space of "childhood" is completely empty and indefinite. The Modern Age discovers it to be a zone of "unlimited determinacy."[12]

## II.

Reflections on children in German literature of the nine-teenth and early twentieth centuries, the theme of this book, eloquently testify to this permanent irritating confusion. This is not only connected with how the literature of the bourgeois age actively participates in society's "discovery of childhood" and, since the second half of the eighteenth century, is capti-vated as never before with a form of existence that, precisely due to its strangeness and eluding conceptual fixation, ap-pears to be eminently poetical. Moreover, these reflections are embedded in the context of a time that for the history of childhood represents in many respects a phase full of ten-sions, controversies, and upheavals, injecting new momen-tum into literary considerations on the incommensurability of the child in the nineteenth century. Discontinuities in the discourse on childhood emerge in varying contexts and they are so pronounced that the threshold to the twentieth century needs, for several reasons, to be classified as a turning-point of epochal significance.

*Firstly*, these developments affect the field of pedagogy and thus the broader social discourse on the child. In this con-text, a movement emerges as part of a gathering massive criti-cism of educational institutions that, imbued with the critical spirit of Rousseau, pursues no less a goal than to revolutionize society through the means of education. As if the cherished seed of a new humanity, the child is to be finally liberated from the clutches of the dark disciplinary powers, which are rebuked for rearing the child into a "mature" subject with the harshness of military drills and failing to give any consider-ation to a development appropriate for a child. The strident opposition to conventional practices, which, starting from the

Romantic criticism of education, finally breaks new ground with the progressive reformist movement in the second half of the nineteenth century, is also situated in the broader context of a socio-political concern that is focused to an unprecedented degree on the child and leads to the ensuing twentieth century being proclaimed the "century of the child."[13] The wellbeing of the child is placed on the political agenda as the "highest duty of sane statesmanship,"[14] which, in the Western cultural sphere at least, has led to appreciable changes in the lives of children and finally to their gaining—at least in part—recognition as social actors in their own right.[15]

*Secondly*, what stands out with respect to the history of the human sciences is how, with their differentiation in the nineteenth century, the epistemic efforts put into understanding the mysterious creature are intensified and a number of new disciplines specializing in children arise. More and more, the strange being, at times now also independently of questions as to whether children can even be educated, becomes the focus of empirical research reorganized to meet the standards of the modern natural sciences and conquer the unknown terrain.[16] Whereas the child of the Enlightenment period becomes a subject of interest in the context of pedagogical and anthropological questions,[17] it now more and more attracts the attention of a science, independently of schooling considerations, that willingly embraces the specific peculiarities of this "epistemic object."[18] Child and developmental psychology, pediatrics and child psychiatry, and later child psychoanalysis, not only assume that a form of existence *sui generis* is to be comprehended, but moreover also claim that their unique subject demands new and special research methods and instruments.[19] On the one hand, this process means that the discursive dominance of pedagogy is gradually relativized over the course of the nineteenth century; on the other, this shift means that the alterity of the child comes into sharper relief and more disturbing aspects of its existence emerge. Diametrically opposite to the visions of the progressive reform pedagogues, who glimpse in their pupils the primordial and naïve natural state in the sense of Rousseau and his Romantic successors, child and development psychologists at the turn of the century such as James Sully, Karl Groos, Stanley Hall, and Karl Bühler come to the conclusion that the child is to be approached "as a savage, strange, perhaps even threatening being that lives in a world scarcely accessible to adults."[20] Oriented on the standard of the "normal" child, genetic psychology also shows a keen interest in development disorders and speech impediments,[21] while psychiatry establishes the category of the "difficult child," focusing on all those odd aspects of a child's life which seem to be outside behavioral norms and demand therapeutic treatment.[22] A perceived infantile destructive urge, lack of empathy, and sadistic cruelty induce criminal anthropology to even consider the child "a born criminal."[23] Having decisively shaped the Romantic ideology of childhood, the image of the innocent angel is now grimly tarnished.

*Thirdly*, this impression consolidates into a stock idea in the psychoanalysis emerging around 1900. With its assumptions on infant sexuality and the "polymorphously perverse disposition" of child desire, Sigmund Freud's scandalizing *Three Essays on the Theory of Sexuality* from 1905 not only erased conventional talk of childhood purity;[24] the theory of the Oedipal conflict also brought into view breaches of tragic dimensions in the fabric of the bourgeois nuclear family which are of socio-historical significance. With respect to the traditional hierarchies of the familial order, psychoanalysis itself can be historicized and considered in the context of a specifically modern "shift in the power relationship between the generations."[25] Read as a symptom of a time of crisis, Freud's narrative of the Oedipal drama appears in an epoch characterized by "political, religious, and literary fantasies of patricide"[26] and an eroding of the paternalistic systems of authority.[27] Psychoanalysis thus expresses a radical reversal in the cultural imagination of the time, the potential patricide shadowing the innocent angel.

*Fourthly*, aesthetics is also decisively involved in this radical change from a Romantic to a modern image of childhood, a turnaround of historical proportions impacting on the sciences, ideas, and the imagination. As Walter Benjamin noted in the 1920s, the caesuras in the discourse on childhood become patently visible in the domain of the arts. Unlike contemporary pedagogues, writers like Joachim Ringelnatz and painters like Paul Klee had "grasped the despotic and dehumanized element in children" and expressed this in their works. Accordingly, Benjamin emphasizes "the grotesque, cruel, grim side of children's life,"[28] which generally lies obscured in the shadows cast by Romantic idealization and is ignored by "meek and mild educators."[29] Instead of elevating the child into an innocent, it needs to be kept in mind that the child has yet to enter the circle of humanity, for it most likely does not innately possess a moral consciousness. Here Benjamin is not only putting up for debate the humanistic foundations of the bourgeois myth of childhood, but also reminding us that the art of Modernism has condensed and co-constructed these ruptures in the contemporary *episteme* of the child. And what is more: the odd formulation of the "dehumanized element *in* children" points to a differential gap, one that opens up as a "hiatus between the unexperienceable realm of the child and access to it," and that the art of the avant-garde seeks to exploit for new aesthetic approaches and techniques.[30] Similar to Freud, who, given the unavoidable "infantile amnesia," defined the early childhood years as much like a scarcely accessible "prehistoric epoch,"[31] the disconcerting moment of childhood in Benjamin's conception is connected to how childhood actually addresses an impassable domain prior to the symbolic order and, as such, obstinately resists representation, as if any discursive consideration of childhood is ultimately condemned to encountering the boundaries of what is expressible and is thus forced to permanently break through linear narrative patterns with leaps and discontinuities. In the ontogenetic perspective, this pertains to the mute beginnings in the history of the subject, while in the phylogenetic sense it relates to the inaccessible origins of the human: as an impassable liminal space *prior* to all cultural markings, "childhood" is not only one of the main themes of modern art, but also a figure of reflection through which aesthetic works negotiate the form of their very own representation.

## III.

As Benjamin sees it, every attempt to translate childhood experience into discourse necessarily remains tentative, approximate, and fragmentary. Accordingly, this book is so organized that it traces a history of literary childhood in the form of closely-related single studies, each of which however picks up the thread anew—and thus takes into account the aforementioned disruptions punctuating the nineteenth century. The focus is on poetological developments in German literature from Romanticism and Realism through to

Modernism, and these are related in turn to the upheavals in the history of knowledge and ideas. The guiding premise here is that aesthetic reflections on the child are not exhausted simply by illustrating, commenting on, or problematizing the social and cultural dynamics at work; it is even more crucial to recognize the complex *interaction* between literary and non-literary discourses on childhood. As a leading cultural medium, since the eighteenth century literature has exerted a decisive influence on the formation and consolidation of an imaginative space that embraces and steers the poetical, epistemic, and practical access to the indefinite entity that is the child. In the bourgeois age, the literary discourse prolif- erates competing images of childhood which not only shape poetic self-reflection but also the social discourse. On the one hand, the Enlightenment-influenced view perceives an *un- formed* being without reason—it is wild, anarchic, driven by instinct, uncivilized, and is more like an animal or an inferior savage who needs to be reared and educated into a human being. On the other hand, following Rousseau, the image of an *unspoiled* form of existence begins to circulate—the child is innocent, unbroken, one with nature, genial, creative, self- active, and indeed needs to be kept away from civilizing influ- ences for as long as possible. Above all the literature of the German Romantics propagates with this idea a veritable "cult of childhood," its impact for the socio-political discourse re- maining basically unabated down to the present day.[32]

As far as the nineteenth century is concerned, it needs to be emphasized that there is no consensus as to precisely what a "child" is.[33] The cultural imagination of the time is anything but homogenous—and that is probably still the case down to the present day. Older bodies of knowledge and ideas exert a continuing influence and overlap with newer imagery and insights. One faction pursues a rather pessimistic anthropology, which, at least in its beginnings, is noticeably influenced by the doctrine of original sin and has no hesitation in demonizing the child as a sinful creature possessing a depraved nature. In contrast, the other faction is inspired by a more optimistic vision of humankind, one that ignites an impulse critical of the respective contemporary culture and eventually idolizes the child as the great hope for a redeemed future.[34] Here we are dealing with "gigantic projections"[35] which are genuinely poetic accomplishments and through which adults not only say something about the Other but also—and above all—about themselves. Beyond these two patterns, which possess a long theological-moral tradition, more differentiated perspectives develop parallel in the sciences, arts, and literature of the nineteenth century, paving the way for the emergence of a post-Romantic discourse at the turn of the century. In stark contrast to the Enlightenment idea that the individual is inherently capable of being educated, and also stridently contrary to the Romantic construction of a naïve natural creature that serves as nothing less than a normative model of the betterment of humankind, the disturbing and unpredictable moments of childhood existence increasingly come to the fore, giving rise to considerable doubt about the fundamental sociability of humans. This book is interested in the literary genealogy of these post-Romantic childhood narratives, starting from the assumption that they are of salient importance for the cultural self-understanding of pivotal questions concerning the modern individual, the bourgeois family, and the politics of education, and moreover that they play a central role in the shaping of a markedly Modernist aesthetics.

# Idylls of Childhood (*Hoffmann—Stifter*)

## I.

In the bourgeois age, the genre of the idyll is coupled with a modern idea of childhood in an unprecedented way. In "Idyll," an article published in the journal *Adrastea* he himself edited, Johann Gottfried Herder notes for example:

> For, in childhood, is not the Idyll-world our sweetest impression? When the spring awakes, we awake, and feel in it the spring of our life; with every flower we shoot up, we bloom in every blossom. The returning stork clappers us, the nightingale and the lark sing us. In the liveliness and the new springing life of every creature, children take a brotherly and sisterly sympathy. Idylls are the vernal and infantile poetry of the world; the ideal of the human imagination in her youthful innocence.[1]

According to Herder, the nexus of idyll and childhood needs to be read in two ways. Firstly, the connection to the philosophy of history in the tradition of Rousseau has to be understood. For while the idyll as a literary genre traditionally envisions an Arcadian primordial time, it also addresses the ideal of a life in harmony with nature at the very origin of human community. Thus, in the phylogenetic sense, childhood is a positively-connoted stage of humanity prior to all culture. Secondly, Herder also sees the rootedness of the idyll in childhood in a less metaphoric sense, by combining the collective image of primordial time with a new way of looking at children. If children live in harmonious union with nature, then the first age of humanity is to be imagined in an ontogenetic sense as the innocent beginnings of the individual. Almost concurrently, in the context of his genre theory, Friedrich Schiller says of the idyll that "[o]ur childhood is the only undisfigured nature that we still encounter in civilized mankind."[2] Like Herder, Schiller also enhances the status of childhood, elevating it to a higher form of existence, one yet to be alienated and corrupted by sophistication, and by virtue of its unbroken naturalness declares it to epitomize the idyllic. In his deliberations on genre in the *Vorschule der Ästhetik*, Jean Paul also considers the "perfect happiness" depicted as idyllic to be "a reflection of your earlier youthful [...] bliss."[3] As these words show, the interweaving of childhood and idyll in the theoretical discourses of art and literature around 1800 circulates with a remarkable constancy, and in such a way that the two concepts become closely entwined—as if the connection were patently obvious—in the field of the cultural imagination down to the present day. Wherever and whenever the sense of security, innocence, and happiness are lost in the collision with a stark and merciless reality, then childhood is definitively over—this is the pattern on which the stories of childhood in the bourgeois age are usually woven. And yet, it has to be kept in mind that the notion of childhood as perhaps the last residue of the idyllic is a genuinely modern experience, and hence has its own history. Two reasons are pivotal to this constellation.

Firstly, it is literature itself that brings the imagery of the innocent child into circulation, and especially interesting here is the genre of idyll poetry since the 1750s. Symptomatic for this development is that, with the emergence of the bourgeois idyll around 1800, the child advances to a favored motif, while in the pastoral poetry of Antiquity and the Early Modern period it is merely a marginal figure.[4] The depiction of a mythical past in a geographically remote Arcadia, familiar from the pastoral poetry of Antiquity and the Renaissance, is replaced by a new topographical model. The rural safe havens of the modern idyll are organized around the focal point of the family, which is demarcated from the rest of society first and foremost through its affective ties. As the idylls of a Bernardin de Saint-Pierre or a Jean Paul show, replacing Arcadia with the space of childhood entails recoding essential elements of the genre. While traditionally the life of the shepherd was still oriented on erotic yearning, the child in the bourgeois age indicates a marked desexualizing of the idyll and represents by virtue of its primal innocence the image of a lost union at the beginning of the ages.[5] Childhood is thus stylized in modern idyll poetry into the sole remaining paradise on earth, and this occurs in concert with the sacralization of an angelic infantility, as the Romantics, following Herder, emphatically propagate—for instance Novalis, who in a famous aphorism proclaims: "Where children are, there is a golden age."[6]

Secondly, the transfiguring of the child is not only a literary but also a social fact, for it is closely tied to the social upheavals of the mid-eighteenth century. Bourgeois culture conceives childhood anew as a sheltered environment, one that has to be sealed off from the pretensions of society by all available means. The modern discovery of childhood thus finds expression in an ongoing isolation of children and an increasing autonomy of their living spaces. To the same extent that the child is exterritorialized, specifically infant spaces are established, and these, separated from those of the adults, are considered by authors like Rousseau or Herder to be residues of Arcadian happiness and symbols of the original paradisiacal and innocent state of humankind.[7] In other words, childhood is imagined as an idyllic *hortus conclusus*, a secluded place, to which adults in principle have no access or at least should not have any access.

These ideas formatively influence the restructuring of everyday social life over the course of the nineteenth century. The private living space is fundamentally changed by the introduction of the nursery, and public space through playgrounds or other universes of play, dividing the world into one for adults and another for children. Similarly, the institutionalization of spaces reserved for children, such as everyday school, boarding school, or kindergarten, proceeds unabated. And precisely the latter example, the kindergarten, the term coined by the German pedagogue Friedrich Fröbel who succeeded in establishing it politically as an institution in the mid-nineteenth century, demonstrates the status accorded childhood in bourgeois culture. In place of the traditional "safe houses for small children," Fröbel propagates in a manifesto from 1840 that the kindergarten be made in the image of the Garden of Eden, reclaiming for the present a niche-like world before the Fall of Man: "As plants are nursed in a garden under God's protection and under the care of experienced, wise gardeners in harmony with nature, so too the noblest plants, humans, are nurtured, children as the seeds and shoots of a humanity in harmony with itself, with God and nature."[8] But to the same degree that this undertaking asserts a more intensive concern for the welfare of children, as its garden metaphoric reveals, it also expresses the view that there is no place in this paradise for creatures to grow up wildly. Like a lovely delicate flower, the nature of the child has to be a compliantly groomed and cultivated one.[9] And in other words, this means: it is only possible to understand childhood as an idyll when massive ideological premises and norms are accepted. Michel Foucault has encapsulated this as follows:

When, with Rousseau and Pestalozzi, the eighteenth century concerned itself with constituting for the child, with educational rules that followed his development, a world that be better adapted to him, it made it possible to form around children an unreal, abstract, archaic environment that had no relation to the adult world. The whole development of contemporary education, with is irreproachable aim of preserving the child from adult conflicts, accentuates the distance that separates, for a man, his life as a child and his life as an adult. That is to say, by sparing the child conflicts, it exposes him to a major conflict, to the contradiction between his childhood and his real life. If one adds that, in its educational institutions, a culture does not project its reality directly, with all its conflicts and contradictions, but that it reflects it indirectly through the myths that excuse it, justify it, and idealize it in a chimerical coherence; if one adds that in its education a society dreams of its golden age [...], one understands that fixations and pathological regressions are only possible in a given culture.[10]

According to Foucault's considerations, two aspects of fundamental significance need to be taken into account with respect to the modern discourse on childhood. Firstly, the institutions of childhood are shaped by an archaizing trait that is to be understood as the social manifestation of a regressive neurosis. Social institutions like the kindergarten are thus not a refuge ensuring an idyllic childhood, but in the first instance express a collective *wish* for an idyllic childhood, a kind of *idée fixe* that, for all else, expresses the dream of a golden age. Secondly, the bourgeois ideology of childhood is tangible as a cultural construct, which to the same degree that it creates a shelter from society produces a gap within the child. With great acumen, Foucault underlines the discrepancy between a "fictive" and a "real" life in modern childhood, a discrepancy that now becomes intelligible as the latent condition for constituting the imagery of an idyllic garden.

Taking up this conflict analyzed by Foucault, in the following I wish to show that in the nineteenth century it is principally literature where the inner antagonism in the bourgeois conception of childhood is played out. When literature spawns childhood utopias like the Cockaigne and remote charterhouses in rural idylls, or other fantastical little countries in total isolation from the outside world, and when it situates children systematically in inaccessible and mysterious places like the "hiding place behind the curtain, the cramped space under the table, the scary/secret basement, the seldom used or prohibited chambers with their specific smells and treasures, the attics with the poetry of forgotten things and bric-a-brac," etc.[11]—then it is reflecting their exclusion from society and the objective irreality of their existence as children. In Modernity, the life of children is formatively shaped by a fundamental bifurcation arising from how they belong at once to the wondersome realm of childhood and the rational sphere of adults. The literary imagination does not propel this dualism to the surface first with the emergence of Realist poetics, however, as could perhaps be expected; rather, it is already clearly discernible at a time when the idealization of childhood is reaching its peak, namely in Romanticism.

To make this diagnosis plausible, two texts, both of which are amongst the pivotal reflections on childhood in nineteenth-century German literature, will be closely analyzed and related to one another: E.T.A. Hoffmann's tale *The Strange Child*, published in 1817, and Adalbert Stifter's story from 1853, *Kazensilber*, which takes up distinctive elements from the Romantic pre-text and reconfigures them under Realist premises into a new constellation. These two stories possess a homologous structure which is of particular interest for the issue under discussion: as both narratives take up and unfurl the idyllic coding of childhood, they simultaneously consider its intrinsic imperilment and destruction—and in a such a dramatic way disclose the ideological kernel of childhood idylls.

## II.

The protagonists in E.T.A. Hoffmann's tale *The Strange Child* are two children growing up in a perfect idyll, Felix and Christ-lieb. As the beginning of the narration tells us, they live with their parents in a tiny village; along with the von Brakel family, only four farmers live there. The rural isolation of the coddled setting offers the tranquil image of a harmonious coexistence between man and nature, while presenting a world wherein social differences, in line with the maxims of bourgeois culture, are non-existent. Sir Thaddeus von Brakel may be of aristocratic origin, but it is emphasized that he lives in a modest house and not in a manor, and his appearance is no different to that of the farmers—his children also have the good fortune to enjoy an untroubled rural childhood, spending most of their time in the wood they seem to know every nook and cranny of.

A disaster descends upon this idyll and the tale tells of its consequences, without, however, what transpires being subsequently allayed by the restoration of the original childhood bliss. In contrast to similar scenes in Novalis—namely the reconciling conclusion to Klingsohr's tale—the devastation wreaked by the disaster is irreparable. Judged by the allegorical substance, the destruction of the childhood idyll is due to the incursion of modern written culture. In the caricaturized aristocratic relatives, who have come to visit from the city, a culture obsessed with the rationalizing mind and characterized by a stilted bookish learnedness and platitudinous enlightenment, appear on the scene, and with them the view that educating children is all that matters when interacting with them.[12] The disciplined city children Hermann and Adelgunde are the exact antithesis to the children of nature, Felix and Christlieb. The former may know a lot *about* nature but they have no experience *of* it. When not sitting quietly learning with their private tutor, they spend their time playing with toys specifically bought for them instead of heading to the wood to play. The realities of a modern city childhood burst into the rural idyll, inevitably and lastingly disrupting it, even if the narrator leaves no doubt as to where his sympathies lie. The allure of the new toys is so great that Felix and Christlieb occasionally forget the wood and the meadow, eventually becoming disturbed and confused. They are also overwhelmed by the sense of being uneducated and ignorant,[13] while, after the visit of the relatives, a private tutor is hired to mentor them, a Master Inkblot who takes sinister pleasure in pricking the children with a hidden needle. The loss of the idyll, with which Hoffmann configures the drama of literacy, is—quite literally—brought to the point as sheer physical pain.[14]

With respect to the formal structure, it is by no means irrelevant that the marvelous first materializes at this point in the story. The fairytale moments take place precisely when childhood happiness is endangered by the intrusion of the prosaic world. It is as if the idyll loses its natural radiance and poetry through the confrontation with the urban-aristocratic culture—Felix and Christlieb are sad and distraught, and the happiness of their days in the wood seems lost forever. One could be led to think that the archaic form of the fairytale serves to compensate the looming threat to the idyll by establishing a fantastic counter world, or at the very least to allay the impact. And indeed at first it looks this way, Felix and Christlieb going to the wood where, at a place remote and charming, they encounter a strange child who, without any name or origin given, unexpectedly emerges from the bushes.[15] Together with this magical being, who opens up a space prior to all cultural markings,[16] they soon relearn how to relate to nature—to sing and play in a way that recalls the innocent naïvety of their recently lost past. As becomes clear, the liaison with the strange child remains exclusively with the children—only Felix and Christlieb have access to a sphere that, while just a few steps from the house, functions according to rules completely different to those of the adult world. But it soon becomes evident that this domain is also under threat, and that Hoffmann's tale is not geared to restoring a world of innocence and peace when this has been lost in factual reality. Instead, the tale absorbs the dangers of the surrounding outside world and creates a child heterotopy, one that is by no means free of fear and terror. The wonderland of a childhood characterized by nature, poetry, and imagination turns out to be unknown and disturbing. "*The Strange Child*—this title ultimately stands for a childhood that is neither 'cozy' nor 'snug,' but alien and disconcerting."[17]

Considering other fantastic stories by Hoffmann, it is no surprise that the otherworld of childhood is imagined as a place where traumatic experiences occur. In *The Sandman* for instance, a harmless old wives' tale turns the bourgeois living room into a gory hell, while in *The Nutcracker and the Mouse King* a cute child in a cradle mutates into an ugly mouse monster. In *The Strange Child* it is a gruesome gnome king called Pepser who haunts the realm of childhood. As the wondrous creature in the wood relates, it comes from a fairy kingdom that would be indescribably beautiful if Pepser had not resolved to target children and threaten them with death by, as the story puts it, dousing everything "with a layer of disgusting black fluid."[18] Via this unmistakable allegory of writing, Pepser is associated with Master Inkblot in the village reality of Brakelheim. Like the evil spirit from the fairy kingdom, Master Inkblot with his pitch-black wig is an antipode to the children. In his capacity as tutor, it is his task to teach Felix and Christlieb the natural sciences; the introduction into culture, as joyless as it is enlightened, goes hand in hand with an irreversible alienation from nature. Not only does Master Inkblot speak about the wild wood with open hostility; he also destroys the world of the children, soon revealing himself to be the gnome king Pepser and scaring away the strange child from the wood forever. And thus, in the end, things are not put right again—even after the father of Felix and Christlieb has managed to expel Master Inkblot/Pepser. Instead of peace returning to the rural idyll, Sir Thaddeus von Brakel dies, so that the aristocratic relatives claim the house and the family, now destitute, is forced to leave the lovely and tranquil little village. At the end, the strange child appears once again and takes all the pain and grief from Felix and Christlieb, enabling them to become glad and happy adults. At the same time though, the text emphasizes that the dream of innocence, harmony, play, and freedom is only a dream—quite simply because a land over which children alone rule does not exist in reality: "Felix and Christlieb succeeded so well in all they did that they and their mother were very happy. And even later they played in sweet dreams with the strange child who came from that marvelous, distant country, and who never tired of showing them all its wonders."[19]

With this, the story becomes understandable as a text that is not just a fairytale for children but tells of childhood itself as fairytale. This fairytale does not represent an idyllic counter world, for it incorporates the confrontation with the prosaic reality of recent times in a kind of *mise en abyme*. Hoffmann's anti-pedagogic attitude, so vividly expressed through the figure of Master Inkblot, continues the Romantic criticism of educational practices, condemning them to be nothing less than a torturous operation exterminating childhood.[20] Facing modern educational institutions, the imagery of the paradisiacal childhood is the glimmer of a regressive vision, which, as Hoffmann sees it, has no foothold in reality. The tale does not, as has been claimed, offer a "conciliatory correction" to the violated idyll.[21] And it does not serve the restoration or the creation of a higher childhood happiness. The fairytale form reflects rather the painful dichotomy children are forced to live with in the reality of "enlightened" societies—the duplicity of their existence namely between an irreal world of childhood and a real world of adulthood.

## III.

Adalbert Stifter relentlessly presses on with this disillusioning of the childhood idyll, directly taking up Hoffmann's fairytale. Parallel to the pre-text, the story *Kazensilber* models a topographical structure, while examining the juxtaposed childhood realm and adult world in accordance with the conventions of Realism. A sense of this is already present in the fact that, like all the stories collected into the *Colourful Stones*,

*Kazensilber* was expressly written for a "young audience,"[22] but in comparison to the intertext is not a fairytale—although fairytale elements play an important role in Stifter's realistic cosmos.

The story revolves around a family living secluded in the country, only leaving the splendid farm in the winter months when they move to their apartment in the city and catch up with what has meanwhile changed in social life there. Following the conventions typical of the idyll genre, the farm is introduced as located "in a remote but very beautiful area" of the country, untouched by the busy goings-on in the city.[23] Lying at the center of the property, the garden, a tranquil expanse in which even apricots and peaches meanwhile ripen, could be called a paradise on earth—if it were not for the mentioning of how devastating storms regularly sweep through and that its very existence is defiantly wrested from the adverse climate. The clever protective measures securing the garden's survival signalize that the harmonious life led in the countryside, seemingly conforming to nature, is from the very outset the result of well thought-out cultivation methods—a distinctive feature of the artificial paradises in Stifter's universe, and thus reminding us that they mask the existence of a permanent threat.[24] All that glitters is not gold—this appraisement of the situation is suggested already in the apt title with its use of mica.[25]

At the same time, the archaic illusion of the idyll is reinforced, the country farm representing the secluded living space of a traditional extended family, made up of a father, mother, grandmother, three children, and the household staff. In contrast, the text characterizes the apartment in the capital as a refuge for the modern nuclear family, only the parents and children leaving the farm in the winter, while the grandmother remains there the entire year with the maids, servants, and farm hands. The allegorical sense of this topographical arrangement is then underscored by the protagonists remaining nameless, the focus placed on their function within the family by referring to their kinship term. As this suggests, the story comments on the bourgeois family discourse, wherein, as has been noted, the new way of life maintains a thoroughly "ambivalent relationship" to the old.[26] In a striking difference to Hoffmann's fairytale, Stifter has the one and the same family move between rural idyll and urban society, so that the ambivalences and the boundaries through which the bourgeois family is constituted in modern society are emphasized. For this reason, Stifter systematically seeks out those insecure peripheral zones where the fabric of the bourgeois family is confronted with what cannot find a place in its hierarchy.

This peripheral zone is approached and explored in *Kazensilber* as a space of childhood. As in Hoffmann's fairytale, besides the city and the secluded farm, there is a third arena. It also appears to be a realm for children and here, too, it is located in wild nature. And in another parallel, it is easily reachable from the quaint idyll of the farmhouse, namely where the "high Nußberg" is,[27] a rocky hill the children often visit when on an outing with their grandmother. Analogous to Hoffmann's fairytale, Stifter's children meet a strange being there, at the boundary to the "settled order,"[28] who one day suddenly emerges from the bushes and with whom the children begin to cultivate privileged contact. Described as a "strange brown child,"[29] the girl in boyish clothing remains nameless and no mention of any origin is made. Obviously she lives far away from civilization, in nomadic homelessness, prior to all affixations posited by culture. The special closeness to the domesticated children is expressed by how she shies away or flees from adults. But here is where the echo of the Romantic fairytale begins to fade, and in a way that is significant for Stifter's conception of childhood.[30]

In contrast to the strange child in Hoffmann, the secret of the brown girl in *Kazensilber* remains to the end. Going by remarks in letters, it appears that Stifter intended to leave open the question of the child's origins, willing to pay the price of "not being understood on all sides."[31] Eluding the grasp of adults time and again, the shy girl marks an insoluble riddle. Significantly, the father of the children, who makes systematic inquiries amongst the rural population and the parish office, also fails to unravel the secret of her identity and origins. Even as the "woods creature"[32] becomes more trusting over time and is integrated into the family household, an irreducible distance remains: in gratitude for miraculously saving the life of the children twice—once during a devastating hailstorm in the woods, and once from a destructive blaze of the house—the parents wish to "educate" her, believing that she can only be happy when living in civilization.[33] But this pedagogic experiment goes awry. As acculturation progresses, the girl becomes—no one knows why—increasingly sad, until she is befallen by illness and eventually vanishes without a trace, never to be seen again. The text thus fails to come up with an answer to the riddle it poses.

In comparison to the intertext, the mystery of the brown girl may be approached as the consequential result of a formal decision, for it signals the most striking difference between the two stories. In Hoffmann's fairytale, the strange child is a creature from a fairy kingdom—a marvelous and eternal child who neither develops nor grows up; the girl in the Realist text, as is to be expected, has nothing of this supernatural aura. She does not perform any miracles,[34] while unlike the fairy child her childhood is finite: she grows up and gets older, entering puberty.[35] At the same time though, Stifter clearly constructs a Romantic atmosphere around the "Nußberg," evocatively connecting it with a whole series of fairytale motifs: beginning with the name of the rocky hill taken from fairytale literature, how the grandmother tells the children fairytales and legends on the outings there, through to the brown girl herself, who with her last words to the family ominously quotes one of these tales told by the grandmother: "Sture Mure is dead, and the high rock is dead."[36] But in a significant distinction from Hoffmann, these fairytale motifs have precisely the status the text itself gives them—they are quoted fragments, no longer possessing the power to construct a magical counter world to profane reality. The children are not entering a fantastic fairytale realm while up on the "high Nußberg," but only hear stories about it from their grandmother.[37]

With this, Stifter is working on a de-Romanticizing of an archaic tradition, one that in the bourgeois culture of the nineteenth century, and by the time of the Brothers Grimm at the latest, is considered particularly suitable for children. Quite radically, he continues a subverting tendency already discernible in Hoffmann and, little by little, corrodes the Romantic myth of the divine child as the sign of a Golden Age, imagination, and poetry. And in the same vein, the secret of the wood creature does not serve a Romantic mystification and exaltation of the primordial child of nature. With the enigma of the brown girl, Stifter is furnishing rather a thoroughly realistic diagnosis—that childhood in the reality of the modern world has indeed become a riddle, one that the story approaches and discusses as nothing less than the enormous gulf now separating the adult world from that of the children.

In the last analysis, with the vanishing of the brown girl Stifter is staging the complete disappearance of childhood in the Modern Age. This is particularly noticeable in *Kazensilber* due to the absence of a genuinely infant sphere. Whereas the wood still serves as an exclusively children's realm in Hoffmann, albeit an idyll that is then disturbed by the incursion of the gnome king, Stifter's children are always accompanied by an adult when they head off to the Nußberg, namely their grandmother. Although she functions as a mediator between the worlds, the children are never alone for even a minute and cannot enter any autonomous space that could be seen as contrastive to the rationality governing the household culture. Moreover, as the parents' attempt to educate the brown girl shows, the children's kingdom in Stifter is one that is firmly occupied by adults—as there is no place for wild children of nature in the disciplining spaces of modern pedagogy, the bourgeois family here is defined by the task of ushering the uncivilized offspring into the space of culture. In accordance with this ideology, the children of the farm in *Kazensilber* embody, from the beginning through to the end, a cultural childhood, one that at no point deviates from the paternal order determined by the dictates of reason. With these dutiful offspring, the traits of alterity unique to childhood seem to be erased—Stifter's poetic universe is "childless" in the sense that it is founded on the normalizing and exclusion of the wild, anarchic, and nomadic.[38]

And thus, the signs under which the connection between childhood and the idyll has been conceived in the literature of the bourgeois age, are now reversed. Whereas the idyll in Hoffmann is still shadowed by the irreversible incursion of culture, it is now a catastrophic nature in Stifter that destroys both the rural peace and the cultural order. The children in the post-Romantic era no longer represent a Golden Age, no longer guarantee even a residue of the idyll. Liminal creatures, they no longer recall the harmonious and pristine origins of humankind, but the perpetual crack which they are forced to live with in the process of socialization—the crack *between* nature and culture, *between* unreason and reason, *between* the world of children and that of adults.

# Christmas

One of the three main festivities of Christianity, Christmas, celebrated on December 25 since Late Antiquity,[1] is marked by a characteristic tension. Celebrating the birth of Jesus Christ has become established as a cultural practice taking place in two spheres, that of the sacred and the profane. Since spreading, at the instigation of most notably Martin Luther, beyond the boundaries of the Church in the Early Modern period, the Christmas festivity leads a manifest double life between liturgy and customs. On the one hand, the Church rite takes place in a sacred space and celebrates the birth of the Christ Child as the pivotal event of salvation history, the event that structures our time and not only recalls but indeed cements its ordering function. On the other hand, the celebration unfolds in the familial intimacy of a domestic milieu that, since the spread of bourgeois culture in the eighteenth and nineteenth centuries, is fitted out according to the rules of a meanwhile very stable code. While this festivity is connected with the nativity story as it is told in the gospels of Luke and Matthew, it obeys very different rules. At the center of the domestic feast is not an eschatological event, but the handing out of gifts to children. Correspondingly, the cultural history of this custom encompasses the origin of the fir tree, the emergence of the toy industry, Christmas baking, and the composition and spread of Christmas carols, not to mention the commercialization of the Advent season, the Christmas market, and the "Christmas trade," which addresses children like no other.[2] In this case however, the gap that opens up between the Church and the bourgeois-economic order is not to be traced back, one-sidedly, to how religion loses its authority in the purportedly so secular Modern Age. The hiatus is rather constitutive for a cultural practice that serves as a kind of switch-point at the transition from the sacred to the profane. Drawing on Giorgio Agamben's concept, the relationship between the popular custom and the Christmas celebration of the Church may be described as a "profanation."[3] Viewed in this way, the sacred is not negated or voided by the secular festivity, but transformed in a specific way. Putting it pointedly: the bourgeois culture of the Modern Age transforms the celebration of the holy child into a celebration of the holiness of every child.

This is in any case the conclusion drawn by a work published in 1806 and penned by the theology professor Friedrich Schleiermacher, entitled *Christmas Eve Celebration: A Dialogue*. Written at a time when the celebration of Christmas begins to establish itself in its bourgeois form, the text registers the significant shift from the Church to the intimate space of the family, which is organized in the Modern period around the emotional focal point of the child. According to Schleiermacher, "Christmas is most appropriately the children's festival,"[4] its main arena lying far removed from places of the sacral in the cozy and atmospherically decorated living room of the home. Here everything revolves around handing out presents to the children, who, as the receivers of these gifts, are placed in the foreground, a situation that evokes a return to the feeling of childhood—"[w]e were young again, felt like children"—and a reminiscing meditation on a time of comfort and innocence.[5] As much as Schleiermacher allows those characteristics of the celebration conveying salvation history to recede, he describes all the more vividly the profanation of Christmas under the incessant influence of the sacralization of the bourgeois family. Based on the model of the "holy family," it is not just the child who is idealized in every respect, its traits directly inferable from the rhetoric used for Christ: "sweet, angelic, heavenly, innocent, sent among humans by God as a supernatural being."[6] Also the father, just like Joseph, is pushed to the fringe of the familial event, enabling steadfast motherly love to come all the more to the fore and shine forth: "in this sense every mother is another Mary"[7] states Schleiermacher's text, encapsulating a principle of bourgeois family ideology. Gradually, all familial positions are elevated into a status of holiness, overwriting the eschatological original text without rendering it completely invisible.

Schleiermacher has repeatedly been understood as the precursor of a Modern or indeed Postmodern conception of the Christmas celebration, liberating it from the interpretational sovereignty of the Churches and opening it to broader appreciation. But even more accurately, he is to be read as an analyst of cultural processes who precisely grasped the structural divergence of the Christmas celebration. Schleiermacher describes the hiatus between liturgy and custom, between sacred festivity and bourgeois celebration as the gap between scripture and performance. This leads to the assumption that the "remembrance of the Redeemer's birth is far better preserved"[8] by the festival than through Bible study and instruction. This unorthodox position does not follow from some theological argument but rather an insight into the nature of media: "Indeed, rites so much more effectively serve this purpose than words that not infrequently it was for the sake of festive rites and traditions, after their true signification had been lost to view, that false histories were fabricated and even came to be believed."[9] Every festivity, the stability it mediates, revolves around an *un*-stable moment. As much as the rites serve to stabilize cultural orders, in their mere performance there slumbers the potential to initiate a break with tradition. In the case of celebrating Christmas, Schleiermacher believes that it owes its broad appeal and importance to how it has migrated from the Church into the home and amongst children. "There is where we ought to fasten down what is valuable and sacred to us."[10] Obviously the secular celebration is about producing a stable setting for something that in the lives of children is in itself uncertain and unstable.

Literature in the bourgeois age, which down to today is brimful with texts on the Christmas story,[11] has frequently emphasized this instability at the very core of the family celebration. Since Goethe's *Wilhelm Meister's Apprenticeship* (1795–1796), Christmas is used as a stage for representing a drama of socialization, namely the bourgeois subject's process of individualization. In a self-reflexive manner, the *Bildungsroman* tells the story of a Christmas gift, a puppet set that the mother gives to her son, motivated by her enthusiasm for the theatre, and thus arouses in Wilhelm the Oedipally-enmeshed desire to become an actor. The giving of a present is the medium of initiation into a social role, one that Goethe sets up as an intricate drama of "individuality" under outside directorship. Subsequently, the literature of the Goethe era describes the latent abysses and dangers lurking behind the child's crossing into the adult world. It is in this spirit that E.T.A Hoffmann's Christmas tale *The Nutcracker and the Mouse King* (1816) tells of a crisis that allows the pathological dimension to shine through the façade of the otherwise idyllic world of the family celebration. At its center is a girl named Marie who, endowed with a vibrant imagination, at night glimpses the dark side of socialization amongst the presents, a battle as marvelous as it is violent and bloody taking place that ends in the painful parting from childhood.

The Christmas celebration and the handing out of presents to children come into relief as a veritable *rites de passage* in the literary discourse, entrusted with the task of organizing a difficult, potentially traumatic introduction into the cultural order. In nineteenth-century German literature, a highpoint of this "poetics of the Christmas festivity" is *Rock Crystal* from the collection *Colourful Stones* (1853), written by an author intimately familiar with the works of Goethe and Hoffmann, namely Adalbert Stifter.

Secondary literature on Stifter has repeatedly conjectured if the novella initially published under the title *Christmas Eve* in 1845 is indeed to be read as a Christmas tale.[12] While one faction focuses on the Christian metaphors and symbols, arguing that the rescue of the children Sanna and Conrad from their desperate situation is to be associated with the miracle of the birth of Jesus, which manifests in the sky as a kind of wonder of light, the other has criticized the reading of *Rock Crystal* as a Christmas story, pointing out that the text addresses a dramatic withdrawal of transcendence, rendered in the imagery of the "blinding whiteness" of a blizzard suddenly engulfing the children and particularly evident in a curt remark by the narrator: "There was no other side."[13] Both readings however have neglected a basic set of facts, namely that Stifter's narrative opens with an extensive consideration of Christian festivities and the story itself is preceded by a small treatise on the essence of Christmas. Unlike Goethe and Hoffmann, Stifter writes a kind of "meta Christmas novella" that, at its beginning, moves on the same level as Schleiermacher's cultural analysis, the reflection structured around the precise separation between the religious and bourgeois festivity, between liturgy and customs steeped in tradition. After describing the rite as practiced in the Church in the opening section, the narrator then focuses on the profane Christmas celebration, which he, like Schleiermacher, sees as arranged around giving the presents to children:

> Associated with the religious festival is a domestic one. In Christian lands far and wide it is the custom to portray for children the advent of the Christ-child—a child Himself, most wondrous that ever dwelt on earth—as something joyous, resplendent, exalted, an ever-present influence throughout life that sometimes in old age, for one lost in sad or tender memories, revives bygone days as it passes on wings of fair colors, through the cheerless expanse of desolate night.
>
> It is the custom to present children with gifts the Blessed Christ-child has brought; given usually on Christmas Eve when dusk has deepened into night. Candles are lit, generally a great many, that flicker together with the little wax-lights on the fresh green branches of a small fir or spruce tree that has been set in the middle of the room.
>
> The children must wait till the sign is given that the Blessed Christ-child has come and left His gifts. Only then is the door thrown wide for them to enter, and the sparkling radiance of the candles reveals objects hanging from the tree or spread out on the table, things beyond anything the children have imagined, things they dare not touch but which, after they have received them as gifts, they will carry about in their little arms and afterwards take with them to bed. If later in their dreams they hear the midnight bells calling the grown-ups to church, *it will perhaps seem to them that the angelic host is winging its way across high heaven*, or that the Christ-child is returning home after visiting children everywhere and bringing to each a wondrous gift.[14]

The domestic celebration of Christmas is described as a carefully staged deception, a maneuver that not only allows the adults, in a display of affection, to give the children presents, but moreover to guide them into perceiving nothing less than apparitions. Emphasizing that the children, entranced, *think* they can see the Christ child in the firmament and not the "cheerless expanse of desolate night," then from the very beginning doubt is cast on the possibility to religiously interpret events to come.[15] As a Christmas tale, *Rock Crystal* is thus not to be read in a sacral but a profane sense.

As in Goethe and Hoffmann, the narrative following the introduction represents a drama of socialization played out in the days over Christmas. It is no coincidence that the two child protagonists are forced to master the challenge of a "crossing"—on Christmas Eve they set off alone from Gschaid to Millsdorf, the path leading over a col separating not only the two hostile villages but the families of their father and mother, respectively. While traversing this "in-between" terrain, the siblings Conrad and Sanna are surprised by the elements, a blizzard causing the children to completely lose their bearings and head in the direction of the forbidding glacier, a terrain with no recognizable landmarks. Here they barely survive the freezing Christmas night in an ice cave before finding their way back to the world of signs and civilization the next day. "They've been over the glacier and the crevasses without knowing it,"[16] remarks the shoemaker, underlining the enormity of the survived danger. Finally relating the return of the fully exhausted and numb siblings to the trusted circle of their family and community, the story unfolds the events so that they receive their gifts next to the tree in the cozy room at home, and only now, not by coincidence, they partake in the bourgeois rite that is supposed to allay the horrors of socialization. The Christmas festivity is thus staged as a custom that does not celebrate a holy event but navigates the children's entrance, as risky as it is precarious, into the realm of culture.

Despite the claims of readings slanted towards the Biedermeier, Stifter's text clearly shows that the gentle absorption of the children into the orders of society and culture is merely superficial. The story brings out into the open the overshadowed and universally distorted fact that this act is nothing less than a co-opting, a taming, and a subjugating of creatures of nature, using economic terms to describe how "[o]nly from that day on were the children really felt to belong to the village, and not to be outsiders. Thenceforth they were regarded as natives whom the people had brought back to themselves from the mountain."[17] What is here vaguely indicated needs to be underscored as pointing to a repressed reverse side of the bourgeois rite, which Stifter only partially conceals with the idyllic tableau positioned at the end of *Rock Crystal*.[18] This repressed aspect will emerge later however in less peaceful versions of the Christmas story. Half a century after Stifter's novella, a patient, who will enter the annals of psychoanalysis as the *Wolfman*, told his famous doctor a dream that has since attracted enormous attention:

> So it was already Christmas in his dream; the content of the dream showed him his Christmas box, the presents which were to be his were hanging on the tree. But instead of presents they had turned into—wolves, and the dream ended by his being overcome by fear of being eaten by the wolf (probably his father) [...].[19]

With this vision of the Christmas tree and the giving of presents to children, Freud bears witness to all those ambivalences, uncanny experiences, fears and anxieties which accompany the process—by no means non-violent—of socialization in the nuclear family, and of which Stifter had already so perceptively told.

# Rescuing Children (*Stifter*)

## I.

Published in 1846 in the almanac *Iris*, Adalbert Stifter's novella *The Forest Wanderer*, frequently seen as a deeply autobiographical work, was the subject of unusually severe criticism in terms of both its form and content. Contemporaries considered the relationship between the individual sections to be so disparate that the patience of readers was unduly taxed. As for the content, the themes dealt with were considered obscure and mysterious at best—while some readers found the text so morally dubious and abstruse that they put it aside.[1] Whether Stifter declined to have the novella included in the collection *Colourful Stones* because of its lack of success is a question that must remain unanswered. What we also cannot explain today is if the rejection by the contemporary public had a lasting impact on the subsequent reception of the text, which has been generally neglected down to the present day.[2] One possible reason for this disregard is that Stifter's literary representation of childhood has attracted comparatively little attention.[3] In contrast to this, I would like to show that *The Forest Wanderer* is the text in Stifter's work that not only explores this theme programmatically but does so with a deeply disturbing radicalness. This is nothing less than a key text, allowing an analytical approach to various problematic aspects of childhood. With this novella Stifter highlights for the first time a topic that often recurs in later texts. In essence, *The Forest Wanderer* addresses four points which correspondingly open up four perspectives: 1) a narratological, 2) a pedagogical, 3) a poetological, and 4) a political. In order to distill a workable structure from Stifter's multilayered depiction, these aspects, which are of general importance for literary reflections on childhood in the nineteenth century, need to be set out, before, in the ensuing principal part, a close reading can furnish the argumentative proof for the thesis formulated above.

Firstly, the intricate narrative displaces the early stage of life into a kind of prehistoric time. This is already evident in how the anonymous first-person narrator says practically nothing about his own childhood when looking back at his early years and instead gives an account of the story of the strange wanderer in the forest. Above all, however, the early memories are characterized by a temporal discontinuity: as the novella progresses it takes up events lying ever further in the past and the narrative connection is abruptly ruptured on several occasions by the additional insertion of back stories.[4] This complex structure not only gives expression to the experience that the work of remembering undertaken in literature is a gradual delving into an elusive and seemingly inaccessible past. The formal features of the text also reveal a dimension out of time, so that childhood, without even the slightest hint of nostalgic sentimentality, points to a pre-symbolic sphere prior to all culture. In Stifter's work, to look back at childhood is to gaze into a different and strange world.[5]

Secondly, the novella reflects the nature of the infant in line with pivotal anthropological and pedagogical questions, with which Stifter addresses Enlightenment thinking. The main character of Georg, the lonesome wanderer in the forest, is presented in the first part of the text as the mentor of a gamekeeper's son growing up on the fringe of civilization, taking charge of the boy's upbringing with the consent of his natural parents. This scenario continues the tradition of an interest in wild children that emerged in the eighteenth century.[6] But as much as Stifter shares this curiosity for the perfectibility of humans, the novella neither rebukes the uncivilized behavior of those still of nonage in the style of an Enlightenment pedagogue, nor does it furnish an anthropological proof of the formability of humans. Because the text strikingly blends out the fate awaiting the boy and, thus, the very outcome of the formative process, attention is directed on the phase of transition. Toiling so arduously to master, if at all, the obstacles to cultural order, the boy is cast as a liminal figure, occupying a genuinely infantile area *between* nature and culture, *between* animal and human, *between* language and non-language.[7] Stifter's focus is neither an original state of nature in the manner of Rousseau, nor a utopian-paradisiacal form of existence as postulated by the early Romantics. Instead, children attract attention in the difficult *process* of socialization, and for Stifter this process is fundamentally open-ended. [8]

Thirdly, the focus on the threshold to a symbolic order concentrates, in a remarkable emphasis, on the feeling children have for language. *The Forest Wanderer* marks education primarily as instruction in the correct use of language. While the boy initially has an immediate relationship to words, whereby no difference is discernible between them and reality, entering the world of culture coincides with adopting a rationally organized sign system. Growing up thus means distinguishing between language and reality in such a way that it becomes possible to establish a clear relationship between them; at the same time, Stifter refrains from a one-sided denigration of children's linguistic incompetence as deficient. As later novellas show, the pre-symbolic and at times even pathologized way of dealing with words proves poetologically relevant for Stifter's work. In *Tourmaline* or *Forest Fountain* for instance, the peculiar language of the gamekeeper boy is taken up and expressly coupled with questions of poetry.[9] Through the figure of the child Stifter explores a kind of archaeology of poetic speech. Alert and sober, by emphasizing an a-mimetic and—following the etymological meaning of *in-fantile*—"non-saying" dimension, Stifter engages the Romantic tradition, which repeatedly located the poetological relationship between childhood and literature in the idealized notion of a natural poetic expression innate to the child. In Stifter's work however, infantile language does not signalize a paradise of poetry, but rather exposes a dimension of speech that is disturbing because it is asocial.

The question of how children can be integrated into the field of language and culture has, fourthly and finally, a political framework that goes beyond the social brisance of pedagogical agendas and impacts on the lives of offspring in an existential sense. Up until now, secondary literature has not been taken into account that argues, with regard to the dominant motif of childlessness in the second part of the novella—only superficially touched on by referring to the biographical detail of Stifter's own childless marriage—that *The Forest Wanderer* relates upbringing and education to the sociopolitical challenges of the time. This discourse comes to the fore at the climax of the plot, in an expansive and pivotal scene, as the tragic dissolution of Georg and Eleonore's marriage is justified with its sterility. As contemporary reception saw it, not without a sense of appalled shock, *The Forest Wanderer* brings into play a scandalous desecration of conceptions which in relationship to the "family" are traditionally metaphysically encoded.[10] These reactions failed to appreciate that Stifter's novella was in fact addressing changes in nineteenth-century social politics: What is a family? What is life? What is a child? These are fundamental questions debated not just in literary texts. As traced by Michel Foucault, the crystallization and entrenchment of a biopolitical modernity at the passage from the eighteenth into the nineteenth century witnessed a shift in the focus of political thinking towards a concern for the sheer physical existence of the population, initiating a rigorous biologizing of human life.[11] To the same degree as the new power nexus sought to enhance and optimize the reproduction of the populace, infertility and childlessness concurrently become key issues because, as Stifter puts in his work on the state, they endanger "the feeding and development of the multitude."[12] In this vein, the child becomes a topic of social concern in *The Forest Wanderer*, and the considerations on procreation and reproduction link into the demographic discourse of the time.

According to Stifter's political view, the state has a vital interest in educating children:

> The human species has to survive, and for this purpose it has to also educate its members. The state is to therefore use its institutions to develop and educate youth, and if its purpose is to promote the welfare of citizens it *must* utilize them [...], and we thus arrive at the standpoint where we, stringent in morals and virtue, make the fatherland indestructible.[13]

As Stifter sees it, the legitimacy of the education institutions is based in no higher purpose than ensuring the continued existence of the human species. In the following, I shall take this up in an effort to identify the internal connection between the seemingly divergent parts of the narrative in *The Forest Wanderer*. As I hope to show, pedagogy and social politics pursue a common goal, namely to rescue children, and this is to be achieved in line with the precepts of modern biopower, not metaphysically but physically.

## II.

In its first part, *The Forest Wanderer* begins as a pedagogic story on cultivating a wild boy. After a detailed description of the countryside around Friedberg in southern Bohemia, evoking an idyllic nature untouched by incursions of civilization, the narrator's memories of his childhood long ago illuminate the mysterious figure of the old forest wanderer. Nobody knows where the man comes from. He is described as a secluded and lonely person, without any clearly identifiable family background, without identity, and without any sort of profession. What distinguishes him is that he continually seeks out nature and roams the forests like a nomad. The local farmers thus simply call him the "forest wanderer"—and the narrator comments that country dwellers, like children, describe things in terms of what they seem to directly represent and their most obviously tangible feature. This seemingly instinctive understanding of language is contradicted by the young boy of the poor gamekeeper family, who joins and accompanies the wanderer of his own accord, forging a special relationship with him. The wild features of the barefooted and bareheaded boy amalgamate in a use of language that dominates the first conversation with the natural father and arouses the forest wanderer's curiosity:

> "What did you build with the wood, Simi," asked the father.
> "Hohenfurth," answered the boy, who looked up at the two men with his large blue eyes.
> "I should tell you that I'm not asking for nothing," said the father to his older companion: "that's all that he builds, nothing but Hohenfurth. When he sets out rows of stones, they're Hohenfurth; when he takes pieces of wood and lays them out to form

a four-cornered or five-cornered figure, then it's Hohenfurth; when he sits down by the fence and the shepherd from the Kienberg houses is close by, he says: 'father, a goat's on the way to Hohenfurth, a ram's going to Hohenfurth, a log's floating to Hohenfurth.'"

"Maybe he liked Hohenfurth so much that it's firmly in his mind," said the walker.

"He's never been there," answered the gamekeeper.[14]

Far from belittling the boy as eccentric,[15] the narrator emphasizes a characteristic of his use of language: the child knows no distinction between word and reality, between name and attribute, between sign and signified. Infantile speech precedes these differences; the boy knows nothing of a place called "Hohenfurth" that exists outside of language. The point here is not that the conventional relationship between signs is playfully dissolved and destroyed, but rather a presymbolic dimension is to be captured, a dimension Stifter will later take up for his own writing at the end of an autobiographical fragment.[16] The pedagogic efforts of the wanderer are thus concentrated on introducing the boy to the conventional connection between word and thing, name and attribute, subduing the infantile imagination and subordinating it to the reality principle.[17]

At first glance, one could think that this project, firmly adhering to the parameters of Enlightenment education, is crowned with success. The boy learns to read and write, he learns to set language in a clear relationship to nature while on walks, and he learns to name various mosses and stones and arrange them into a meaningful order.[18] But the end of this pedagogic story broaches the deeper sense of education, which the text questions as doubtful from the outset.

Although he has eagerly learnt everything, the boy seems puzzled and asks: "[...] why is there reading and writing, which I'm now very good at, but I can't do anything with?"[19] On this question hangs everything that eighteenth-century pedagogy seeks to prove through the object of fascination that is the savage child: nature is malleable and it is possible to turn an inchoate, affect-driven, and to a certain degree animal-like creature into a civilized and rational human. Sharing this view with the pedagogue Stifter, the wanderer is also committed to this project, but the narrative conspicuously leaves it open if the boy will continue on and follow the mapped-out path to the end.[20] With its peculiar tautology, the answer of his teacher also leaves a lot to be desired: "[you learn to read and write] so that you can learn more in the future, [...] but you don't understand that yet."[21] Because the child promptly affirms this lack of understanding, and thus shows that he cannot grasp a deeper sense of his education, the pedagogic story of the domestication of the savage boy is characterized by an unfulfilled promise.

Before the narrative sends the boy out into the wide world and loses sight of him, the first part concludes with a highly significant convergence between the pedagogical perspective and family politics. Not only does the boy gradually stop calling his mentor "cousin" (*Vetter*), addressing him instead, as if it were a play on words, as "father" (*Vater*), but education and family are also interlocked by the wanderer holding out the prospect that the boy, as the final goal of his education, could one day write a letter to his mother. This coupling is important because it emphasizes the necessary connection between family and extra-familial education, thus reflecting Stifter's political understanding, which takes the development of rational and free-thinking persons to be the decisive foundation for renewing society[22] and regards the family anchored in civil society to be the nucleus of the large family called the "state."[23] The connection is also relevant because the literary text, beyond the programmatic opinions of its author, casts an ambivalent shadow on literacy and education and gives a bleak diagnosis on the current state of the modern family. In the light of the novella, Stifter's optimism seems very brittle: as the boy's schooling leads him to leave his parents and thus the wanderer forever, the integration of the wild boy into culture goes hand in hand with an inevitable disintegration of the family. In this sense the mentor says to his pupil:

> "My child", answered the walker, "you'll live far longer than I will, and you'll go away before I die, and you'll have to live on alone. Children don't even stay with their own parents, let alone other adults; everyone goes away sometime to conquer the world, leaving behind their parents, even if they have sacrificed so much, and given happiness and their whole heart. It is a law of nature."[24]

With these words the text not only anticipates the outcome of the story, which, after the boy departs, ends with the wanderer leaving the village shortly afterwards and mysteriously vanishing, never to be seen again. They also link into the political framework of the novella.

At the end of the first chapter, a figure appears who is an exception to this alleged law of nature, and thus deserves to be looked at more closely. The family of the knacker Adam, the final encounter the boy and the wanderer make together, represents the now unlikely case that children do not leave their parents. This phenomenon is explained by referring to the life led on the margins of society by knackers; with almost no contact with the rest of the population, there is little opportunity for them to leave the family circle. They "prefer to be at home amongst their own [...], and do what the family has done for years."[25] And not just the name but the old age of Adam, who with his ninety-seven years sits on the bench in front of the hut in the company of his seventy-three-year-old son, reinforcing the image of an indissoluble genealogical unit, points back to a time that seems archaic. The social exclusion of the knackers, denying them access to education and public offices, resonates with the backwardness of a pre-modern epoch. As the trade responsible for removing and rendering the carcasses of useless livestock animals, knackery is considered a disreputable and dishonorable profession at the beginning of the nineteenth century, and thus takes place strictly outside the social fabric of communities. Knackers are gradually included into society from 1819 onwards; they are permitted to join guilds and business is placed under official authorization and subject to police control.[26] Typical for modern politics, this change is part of the process whereby the law installs a new access to the body and life. In the age of classical sovereignty, the knackers' lack of rights stems from how they trade with the "bare life" of animals and operate outside juridical regimens.[27] Knackers, the carcasses they work with, and the resulting products are then all subsequently integrated into the legal context as a way of optimizing the economic benefits: firstly because such menial work is now considered in terms of its functionality, and secondly because "bare life" is recognized as a valuable commodity. Stifter's narrative thus illuminates a marginalized sector of society, linking a historical diagnosis on the state of the modern family to a biopolitical perspective. The interest in the exception of an intact family bond, which contrasts with the desolate state of current conditions and witnesses the irreversible decay of traditional communities in an age marked by modern education and mobility, is—through the figure of the knacker—at the same time oriented on the tense relationship between law and life on the biological threshold of modernity.[28] And thus the core issue is broached that determines the next section of the text.

## III.

Related in the second chapter and finally giving the mysterious protagonist a name and background, the wanderer's biography is from the outset clearly linked to procreation and reproduction. Georg's life story, set far away in northern Germany, is introduced in such a way that it reveals certain parallels to that of the boy. Not only are both of them born into families living secluded lives, but as the narrator underlines at the very beginning of the section, Georg and the boy came into the world only "after a long infertile marriage"—they are thus both the unexpected fulfillment of a long-cherished wish for a child.[29] In retrospect, the special relationship between the two becomes understandable through how Georg's life story explicates something that the wanderer can only convey in the form of a secret fear for the small boy. But above all, a concern for childless couples emerges, already indicated in the first part as the sterility of the Simmi family is mentioned, but now carrying more weight because the whole biography of the wanderer revolves around the question of reproduction.

Unlike the boy, Georg is born into an educated family and lives a modern life. The parents are not from a place of untouched nature but live in a region created by clearing a forest and so defined as a cultural area. A pastor's son, Georg grows up sealed off from the outside world, but is taught with the goal that, befitting his rank, he eventually leaves the parental home "to learn and, like his father, to become somebody."[30] Without any recognizable sign of pursuing his own wishes, Georg moves to a university town to study the natural sciences, keeps himself "healthy by doing physical exercises," all because he is "instructed to do so."[31] He sinks into complete loneliness a little later when his parents die. After the reader is told that his "shy, reticent" nature takes on something "wild" and he, "a spirited isolated man," finally becomes a master builder, at the age of thirty he meets the beautiful Eleonore Elisabeth Corona.[32] The fate of the girl is also related: she has parted from her wealthy parents to marry Georg against the will of her father, and by virtue of this step is characterized as having the air of "desolate grandeur."[33] The marriage of the two eccentrics, appearing as an "enclosed contrast to the rest of the normal world,"[34] could be described as happy if it were not for the fact that it is still childless after thirteen years. The situation leads Eleonore to demand the dissolution of the marriage. But before managing to get her way, she gives a long speech that puts forward an astonishing argumentation:

> "Please listen to me, Georg, I've considered this carefully over the last few days, and in the past as well, and I've not come to speak to you until I believed that the idea had jelled that it seemed right to me, and that I could explain it to you. We have only one life to live. And in this life we should, before God, fulfill the whole cycle of human obligations and joys. The first one is always that a person should be human in the fullest sense. [...] You're almost that, Georg, you've followed your wonderful inner wish, but you've never sold yourself, and along with your craft you've been a strong, free, good person, a person who looked elsewhere than only in their profession. And that's why I became so fond

of you straightaway, you're almost a complete human, Georg, except where circumstances fail you—but perhaps for only as long as we want. One of the first, if not the very first rights of a person, and one of the noblest obligations, is to have children; it's why God has tied the two sexes together in such a joyous way, there is nothing more joyful, unless the feeling of parents may be even sweeter, and the obligation they bear grows even firmer in the heart: we see how, when they have children, that even the crudest people push everything else in the world to one side and serve their children—even to the point of endangering their own lives, they do anything to save the lives of their children, so tremendous and powerful is the drive that dictates that young life live on and the old pass away that has brought forth the young and fulfilled its purpose. [...] It is a great, weighty, sacred obligation that a person, who has only one life, uses it to the full, and takes hold of the means, both human and given by God, to let the world thrive in microcosm through their children. I believe that's why our Church has provided for dissolving marriage so that a falsely entwined bond can be annulled and what was lacking can be replaced again. [...] It is not inconceivable that we will still be granted the blessing of a child. Whatever we have achieved with our marriage, whatever we have given each other, *one* purpose, the main purpose has not been reached. That's why I'm proposing, Georg, that we separate of our own accord, that each of us be unattached again, and if it seems right, to enter into a new union, which may well reward us with the good denied hitherto. [...] Such an act doesn't seem merely allowed to me, it seems right [...]."[35]

Eleonore's remarks have very little in common with the sacred status of the family usually associated with Stifter. Her observations seek to justify separation by claiming that the paramount and sole purpose of marriage is to have children. Although the story subsequently tries to make this reason seem absurd, it is by no means abstruse when we consider the contemporary discourse. The *Prussian Civil Code* from 1794 for example, which pioneers comparatively liberal and strictly secular divorce law,[36] shows that her standpoint is certainly plausible and logically consistent. She not only repeats the opening paragraphs of the marital law almost verbatim, which declare curtly that the "main purpose of marriage is the begetting and upbringing of children,"[37] she can also sidestep the juridical institution of marriage with an out-and-out biological argument because, following the Prussian reforms, childlessness had become an established reason for divorce in the Protestant context around 1800.[38] This historical context shows that the protagonist's argument is anything but "strange and false," as has frequently been claimed. Instead, we have to recognize that her speech testifies to the powerful impact of a demographic thinking, characteristic for the Modern Age, which individuals obviously found difficult to withstand.

Social science of the nineteenth century discovers the family as one of the key issues facing population policy.[39] Here ideas prevailed which are almost identical to those in Eleonore's speech. In Wilhelm Heinrich Riehl's *The Natural History of the German People* (1851–1869) for example, the "idea of humanity" is first fulfilled in the bond of matrimony between husband and wife.[40] After the institution of the "whole household" has increasingly become less important, the nucleus of father, mother, and children is "the first and most intimate sphere within which our full human nature comes to expression."[41] The notion that the family forms "something sacred," invoked by Eleonore on several occasions, explicitly translates the religious into a "social and political" sense in Riehl's work.[42] This shift resonates in Lorenz von Stein's *System der Staatswissenschaft* (1852), where the family is presented as "the vital nucleus of the whole population, for it ensures the proliferation of the population and hinders its decline."[43] Albert Schäffle pointedly defines the bond of marriage as an "organ for the reproduction of the population" or a "unit feeding and reproducing the population."[44]

The debate Stifter raises in the context of these ideas is the sober reduction of the family to its reproductive function.[45] In the light of this radical biologizing of human life, the essence of human beings and the family is not only attained through its own reproduction, but Eleonore's words are also characterized by a strict tenor when defining a "child." The degrading of adoption vis-à-vis natural conception is once again due to the impact of modern biopower:

> And when you, as you once said, adopt the lad of the traveling carpenter who died, then remember that adopted children are not your own. Whoever takes on an obligation without being able to produce the foundations for this very obligation, they create an imbalance that one day takes vengeance. Be kind and do good things for him, look after him, but do not demand that he is your son. [...] Georg, you can only obtain a child in the way I've explained. [46]

What is decisive here is to appreciate that Eleonore is not expressing some unusually strong desire for a child that irreconcilably conflicts with a love she feels.[47] As the advocate and agent of a contemporary discourse that considers the formation of the family to be the fulcrum and nucleus of social and welfare politics, she is not pursuing some private wish but a social objective.[48] For the rest of the novella, we need to keep in mind that this project, no matter how questionable it may seem, determines the actions of the figures.

While at first it may seem as if Georg would take an opposite standpoint, doubting the legitimacy of Eleonore's decision, he eventually approves of divorce. For his part, the narrator also condemns the mutually agreed separation with uncharacteristic bluntness. Firstly, he does so indirectly in terms of plot: Georg goes on to marry another woman with whom he has two children, whereas Eleonore proves incapable of putting her words into action, as she is forced to tearfully admit several years later as the former couple accidentally meet again. Secondly, the narrator's judgment is explicit, stating that the couple has erred and it would have been better for them to stand before God with the "warmth of their hearts" instead of with children.[49] But such a metaphysically-oriented end is put into perspective on several occasions over the course of the narration. Upon taking a closer look at the text, it becomes clear that Georg has in fact followed the secular arguments put forward by his wife to an extent that goes beyond merely consenting to her wish for divorce and, moreover, at no point does he challenge the biological encoding of the concepts of "family" and "child." He puts Eleonore's instructions into practice in a way more befitting an eager school pupil: Once the separation is completed, he enters into a purely functional union and has children. After the death of his second wife and both sons have gone their own way, without maintaining contact with their completely isolated father, Georg also follows Eleonore's ideas by taking responsibility for the upbringing of the gamekeeper's boy. Although it may seem as if the wanderer adopts the child, compensating for the disintegration of his own family, Georg does not consider the child his own. He has accepted Eleonore's doctrine that no adopted son can replace a biological one.

Viewed from this perspective, Georg's education of the boy also needs to be understood in terms of its social significance. With the forest wanderer, the text places special emphasis on a figure who, in agreement with the political goals of the author, shares the concern of integrating every individual into society. Georg tries to achieve what the gamekeeper's family cannot—through education to integrate those on the margins into modern society and, as it were, "rescue" them for the good of the community.

*The Forest Wanderer* is the first story in Stifter's work that brings into play the motif of rescuing children. When Eleonore refers to the primordial drive that sees parents do anything "even to the point of endangering their own lives, [...] to save the lives of their children,"[50] then it is pivotal to see that the instinct that makes parents willing to sacrifice their own life to protect that of their offspring is coupled on one argumentative level with the obligation to reproduce. Against the backdrop of this significant connection, the semantics of "rescuing and saving" is given a genuinely modern stamp in Stifter's work. The conception does not refer to the traditional theological dimension of redeeming souls, but is concerned exclusively with the sheer physical survival and continued existence of the human species. By inserting the rescuing of children into the framework of demographic arguments, the novella makes it clear that not only propagation and reproduction serve to increase population levels. Rescuing children also is subject, in a very basic sense, to the principle of sustaining life, and a pivotal task given the omnipresent risk of death, the minimization of which is one of the central missions of the secular Modern Age. Stifter thus links into a comprehensive politics of rescuing children that had begun to emerge at the end of the eighteenth century. With the goal of turning formerly miraculous redemption into calculable politics and securing, wherever possible, the physical welfare of all members of society, "life saving" organizations and associations spring up like mushrooms and pass all kinds of decrees calling for "the salvation of the unfortunate," resulting in a broad spectrum of "rescue services."[51] The aim to protect life at any price to ensure population growth goes beyond measures introduced to combat direct threats and leads to the founding of institutions with a prophylactic function. Wilhelm Riehl for instance mentions the rapid increase in the number and type of shelters (*Rettungshäuser*) since 1800, i.e. institutions that take in "the urchins found in the streets," educating them with a view to their (re-)integration into society.[52] We can thus see how Eleonore's upholding of the principle of reproduction and Georg's education of the boy who has grown up "behind the hedge" converge in the motif of rescuing children—they share the unconditional concern for the biological existence of *all* individuals, even if it means paying the price of private happiness.

*The Forest Wanderer* admittedly limits its scope to broaching the theme of saving children without depicting the usual scenarios of misfortune and disaster. However, the hope that through education the boy can become a useful member of society and thus safeguarded in the sphere of culture before the myriad dangers become manifest, points to a preventive logic evident in Stifter's educational stories. Accordingly, *The Forest Wanderer* may be read as a pre-text for the novellas of the *Colourful Stones* written shortly afterwards, which are more or less about the miraculous saving and rescuing of endangered children. If we consider these texts in terms of the long tradition of "misfortunate children," then it becomes clear that they depart from the pre-modern version of this genre and pursue, imbued with the spirit of Enlightenment pedagogy, a propaedeutic goal.[53] Stifter's gentle mentors, for example the grandparents in *Granite* and *Rock Crystal* or the priest in *Limestone*, are modern patron saints who, no longer promising miracles, count on education and moral stories in helping the children to learn how to protect themselves from errors and dangers. And even where Stifter plays with the connotations of a metaphysical story of salvation, as is so clearly the case in the story *Rock Crystal*, first published under the title of *Christmas Eve*, the children cannot trust a redemptive Christmas mystery, well aware that there is no "other side."[54] Instead, the skill of the siblings who get caught in a blizzard, hopelessly lose their bearings, and survive the ordeal in the icy mountains thanks to a clever and sparing use of their reserves of coffee, reveals that Stifter's children have to cope with an inevitable forlornness on their own and indeed learn to save themselves.

# On the Threshold of Writing
## (*Rilke—Walser—Benjamin*)

## I.

The work penned in 1844 by the Frankfurt internist and children's book author Heinrich Hoffmann for family use, soon to gain fame internationally under the title of *Struwwelpeter* (English: *Slovenly Peter*, or *Shaggy Peter*), provides an exceptional reflective space not only with respect to the immediate historical, social and cultural context, already the subject of a plethora of studies,[1] but also for the literary history of childhood in the nineteenth century. Significantly, the author signed the first publication with the pseudonym "Reimerich Kinderlieb" (literally: "Rhyme-rich Child-love") and, in the spirit of this self-understanding, he certainly did not see himself as a pedantic pedagogue. The *Struwwelpeter* stories, both textually and pictorially, indeed possess an abundance of micrological details, scarcely covered in research; moreover, beyond the strident educational orientation, they bring to attention disturbing aspects of childhood in such a way that the "little heroes" are ultimately revealed to be "decay products of Romanticism's myth of childhood."[2] Wild and increasingly alien-like in their confrontation with the world, Hoffmann's children mirror not just the dismal state of the bourgeois educational apparatus; the disenchanted idyll also impacts upon the bond—a *topos* since the eighteenth century—between children and literature, according to which the poet-child of genius was rooted in an idea prevalent in the philosophy of history, namely that of a paradisiacal natural being. Having exerted considerable influence as a poetological figure,[3] this relationship now undergoes a reconfiguration that emphatically points the way to Modernism.

One of most enigmatic episodes of *Struwwelpeter* is the "Story of the Inky Boys," which draws its motifs from E.T.A. Hoffmann's tale *The Strange Child*. The action is easily summarized: three boys called Edward, William, and Caspar tease and laugh at another boy because he is "as black as ink," and as a consequence of this act of discrimination are put on trial before a kind of court.[4] Saint Nicholas—in an unmistakable direct reference to "Master Inkblot" from the Romantic fairytale—appears with "mighty inkstand" and authoritatively warns the children to be tolerant, before dunking the obstinate boys over their heads into the black liquid in punishment. Saint Nicholas leaves the scene and one sees how the pitch-black "inky boys," unmoved, continue to ridicule the "black-a-moor" and,[5] together with him, enter a world sealed off from and impregnable to adults. As in all the *Struwwelpeter* stories, the punishment misses the mark, its failure as a pedagogical method is drastically exposed, while the impact is revealed to evince the very opposite of its intention.

In spite of this, the story of the inky boys—and along with it the *Struwwelpeter* overall—has been repeatedly read as a document, typical of the time, from the history of *poisonous pedagogy*.[6] A dark chapter of bourgeois upbringing, Hoffmann's children's book has served to illustrate the strict disciplinary methods employed in modern educational institutions, i.e. in schools and families of the eighteenth and, above all, nineteenth centuries. The tall Saint Nicholas is seen, to draw on Michel Foucault, as a representative of an authoritarian and repressive disciplinary power serving the "'penalty of the norm'" and entailing the matching sanctions[7]—the master's task is to instruct the naughty children in tolerant behavior,

FIG. 1: Heinrich Hoffmann, *Story of the Inky Boys* (1846).

employing admonishing words before then meting out physical punishment. However, the juxtaposition, spread across two pictures, of word and deed, of verbal rebuke and mute violence, is one of surface appearance only, for Hoffmann in fact links the two scenes through an affinity of media. While the children in one picture are reprimanded by spoken words, the other shows them being dipped into the ink, which in terms of

FIG. 2: Heinrich Hoffmann, *Story of the Inky Boys* (1846).

the trope refers to written language. Both pictures are placed into a relationship that is like two facing mirrors: in both cases the disciplinary sanctioning—using the voice, then the written word—is literally carried out as a single word-act. At the end of the nineteenth century, pedagogy employs the notion of "punishing words" as a *terminus technicus* for this practice,

FIG. 3: Heinrich Hoffmann, *Story of the Inky Boys* (1846).

which it puts as a disciplining method on equal footing with other measures such as "natural punishment," prohibitions and deprivations, or physical chastisement. In 1897, the privy councilor to the Prussian Culture and Education Ministry, Adolf Matthias, compiled a small typology of such *punishment techniques* and stated in a remarkable formulation that the

Du siehst sie hier, wie schwarz sie sind,
Biel schwärzer als das Mohrenkind!
Der Mohr voraus im Sonnenschein,
Die Tintenbuben hinterdrein;
Und hätten sie nicht so gelacht,
Hätt' Niklas sie nicht schwarz gemacht.

FIG. 4: Heinrich Hoffmann, *Story of the Inky Boys* (1846).

possibilities to reprimand using words are "as manifold and abundant as our German language is rich in turns of phrase."[8] Certainly unintended, the implication of this statement meets up with the point made by the two pictures of Saint Nicholas in *Struwwelpeter*, and amounts to saying that punitive force is potentially inherent to each and every word. This is symbolically represented in the story of the inky boys: as large and powerful as Saint Nicholas may appear, the inkpot and quill tower over him and emerge in their mythical autonomy as symbolic representatives of power and authority. Baptized as it were in the ink, the boys are not only punished by Saint Nicholas but are also confronted with a structural violence that is coupled to entering the domain of writing.

With this sensitivity for the transition on the threshold to the symbolic order, *Struwwelpeter* anticipates a number of writing scenes in German literature around and after 1900 depicting the child's delicate entrance into writing and script. Following and at once revising the Romantic paradigm, which glimpses the higher purity of the poetic word in the child,[9] literature at the turn of the last century takes part in a project, spanning several discourses, to find new ways of exploring the realm of childhood. Authors like Rainer Maria Rilke, Robert Walser, and Walter Benjamin are not only deeply influenced by the ambitious intentions of progressive reformist education, which around 1900 propagated the emphatic liberation of the child from the clutches of the dark disciplinary powers, but moreover the literary discourse itself absorbs scholarly interest in the prehistory of language and writing, encapsulated by the still young discipline of developmental psychology, with its studies into how children acquire language and learn to write.[10] Without any idealization, Modernist literature cautiously approaches the realm, so difficult to access, "before representation"—following the etymological sense in the Latin word *infans*, it sheds light on a primarily "non- or unspeaking" being, recalling the simple but often forgotten fact that the subject first comes into the world when it leaves behind its original muteness.[11] Drawing on Giorgio Agamben, it may be assumed that the non-speaking beginnings persist however, as lacunae *in* language[12]—it is this constitutive and untamable linguistic exterritoriality of humans that Modernist literature returns to when it speaks of the child.

## II.

In 1900 the feminist and pedagogue Ellen Key publishes in Sweden a book with the prophetic title *The Century of the Child*. Its impact as an "epochal starting point of an aesthetic phenomenon"[13] will also reverberate through German literature. Against the background of a whole spectrum of alternative education projects at the end of the nineteenth and in the early twentieth centuries, Key's study articulates a criticism and is, at the same time, itself a symptom of a crisis: drawing on Nietzsche's turn away from humanist education theory and practice,[14] Key aims her criticism at traditional "flogging pedagogues" and sets a milestone for the progressive agenda.[15] Starting from the "divine character of the continuation of the race"[16] and directly tying in to studies on eugenics by Galton, Spencer, and others, Key, using a Darwinist vocabulary, calls for the "laws of natural selection" to hold sway and that "the punishments of society" be recast into protective— instead of punitive—measures.[17] Envisioning nothing less than the creation of a new humanity,[18] this pedagogy aims to teach a different understanding of child individuality. In response to the crisis plaguing education at the end of the nineteenth century, the progressive movement shifts the focus, its program instructing educators more than the children, so that the guiding methodological principle is: "For success in training children the first condition is to become as a child oneself."[19] This postulate is bound to a fundamental uncertainty and defines the blind spot of progressive pedagogy. The unbroken optimistic hopes pinned to the new century depend namely on a more precise answer to the still unresolved question as to the specific nature and perspective of the child. "The real nature of children," concedes Ellen Key, still needs to be studied.[20] And this brings to an end the attempt to liberate the child from the clutches of the old pedagogy, with the—measured by its own lofty goals—dubious plan to place the child in the crossfire of research. Without the slightest hesitation, Key allies her project with burgeoning child and experimental psychology and speaks of the "transformation of pedagogy into psycho-physiological science."[21] While the path of progressive pedagogy may aspire to guide children out of the old classroom, it certainly does not directly lead them to freedom; they have first of all to pass through the experimental laboratory.

The German translation of the work—*Das Jahrhundert des Kindes*—is published in 1902 and becomes an instant success. The young Rilke writes an enthusiastic review the same year, celebrating Ellen Key as "the child's advocate and apostle" and joining her cultural diagnosis: the child is in a state of "slavery" and must be liberated.[22] As with the Swedish reformer, Rilke's conception of childhood is still very much characterized by the Romantic *topos* of the artist-child. Possessing genuine spontaneity and creativity, its ingenious imagination is the original source of artistic activity, a wellspring that needs to be uncovered and fostered. This idea persists throughout Rilke's early writings. In the same year of 1902 for example, in an essay on his stay in the colony of Worpswede, tucked into the idyllic north German countryside and founded by artists involved in the life reform movement, he enthusiastically underlined the affinity between the artist and the child: both have a mode of existence intimately close to nature and untainted by any attitudes imposed by civilization—the child harmoniously blends with nature instead of seeking to master it.[23] Ultimately, the Rousseauian dream of infantile natural beings forms a utopian endpoint demanding a new vision of the child, which Rilke formulates in terms resonate of Ellen Key: "One must begin to proceed from the child, not from the standpoint of the adult, who knows so little about the child."[24]

For Rilke, these words formulate nothing less than a literary program. At the same time however—and this is pivotal to his poetics—he soon distances himself from the ideal of the primordial artist-child. This is not only evident in how the initially friendly relationship to Ellen Key begins to cool off in 1906 with his pivotal stay in Paris and the commencement of *Malte*, Rilke increasingly judgmental towards the Swedish reformer;[25] it also becomes clear that the project to adopt the perspective of the child is surveyed in all its aporiae and ambiguities. The stage where for Rilke the reformist enthusiasm abruptly dampens, is a significant incident from the Salpêtrière in Paris. While waiting in the corridors of the hospital, Malte Laurids Brigge hears the direct consequences of a scientific project investigating the child's unique character:

> Suddenly, right near me, I heard the screams of a terrified, struggling child, one scream after another, and then a low, suppressed sobbing. While I strained to find out where this sound was coming from, there was again a little scream, and I could hear voices questioning, a voice whispering orders, and then some kind of machine started, and hummed on indifferently. I remembered that half-wall, and realized that all these sounds were coming from the other side of the doors and that the doctors were working there now. [...] Behind the wall, the machines made a pleasant, mechanical hum; there was nothing upsetting about it.
>
> But suddenly everything was quiet [...]. A machine rattled, and immediately stopped; words were exchanged; then the same energetic voice ordered: "Dites-nous le mot *avant*." Spelling it: "A-v-a-n-t" ... Silence. "On n'entend rien. Encore une fois: ...".[26]

What Malte hears once the cries of the children, the voices of the doctors, and the clattering of machines have subsided, is clearly the horror of some initiation. The children are commanded to spell—of all words—"avant," in effect demanding that they perform a double movement, one that leads both "back" and "forward": in the psychophysical experiment they are forced to dissect words into meaningless units and revert to a state prior to language, from where they are to repeat entering into language.[27] For Rilke, "childhood" designates a precarious liminal experience: on the one hand, the child is in a realm *prior* to language ("a-v-a-n-t"), about which it is impossible—at least not directly—to speak;[28] on the other hand, all that can be said is that a child is oriented *forwards* ("avant"), towards the symbolic. A genuinely distinguishing characteristic of children is that they do not yet have language, but unlike adults, possess the capacity to acquire language.

The scene from the Salpêtrière in Paris makes clear that "childhood" in Rilke's work cannot be approached and interpreted biographically—although still a widespread practice—by focusing on his difficult childhood with his mother and in military school or by relying on his strict rejection of psychoanalytical remembrance work. On the contrary, since Rilke commenced work on *Malte* (1906) and the *New Poems* (1907), the possibility of accessing and capturing childhood through language needs to be placed in a systematic relationship to his work in general.[29] In a piece from 1914, programmatically entitled *Memory*, that remained uncompleted and unpublished in his lifetime, Rilke creates a scene marking the start of his writing, motivated precisely by this inaccessible and elusive childhood:

I repeat: I find it quite comprehensible that those who have to depend entirely on themselves, upon their own life's usefulness and bearableness, should feel a certain relief, if there is induced in them a spiritual nausea which enables them to rid themselves piece-wise of the misunderstandings and indigestible experiences of their childhood. But I? Am I not, indeed born to form angels, things, animals, if need be, monsters, precisely in connexion with such experiences, which were beyond experiencing, were too big, too premature, too horrible? Precisely this, O my inexorable God, was what you demanded of me and called me to do, *long before I was of age (weit eh ich mündig war).* And I sat up in my forlorn hospitable bed, beside which lay the uniform of my cadet years, folded with meticulous care, and wrote at Thy command and knew not what I wrote.[30]

Explicitly rejecting the "talking cure" of psychoanalysis, Rilke refers to a kind of primal scene of his literary creativity, which appears to circle unwaveringly around the unsaid of his childhood—not so much in the sense that he reveals his work to be the poetic figuration of an inexpressible stage of his early life, strongly influenced by military school, but rather in the sense of its aesthetic production, setting the beginnings of writing long before he was of age and still the inhabitant of an "in-fantile" ("un-mündig") distant past. In the fragment Rilke recalls the prehistory of his writing, all the more powerful because of its muteness, which only seems to follow the model of inspired creativity. Whereas for Rilke, "writing" means the mechanical "writing down" at the command of another voice[31]— in other words, Rilke's writing is acutely aware of the subject's original in-fantility. Like the children in the Parisian language laboratory, it is not a higher message that comes into focus, but the exterior of the signifiers in their sheer materiality, for the dissecting of the words into their meaningless components in the psychophysical experiment shows that childhood can only ever be approached gropingly and never fully apprehended; it cannot be positively comprehended when proceeding from the symbolic, and only remains present as a loss, i.e. in negative form. The original absence of language reverberates in the lacunae without semantic content between the written letters. With his poetics of childhood Rilke identifies and discloses the blind spots of progressive pedagogy—in contrast to Key's project, the infantile perspective remains structurally inaccessible: "O childhood, o likeness gliding off" bewails an early poem entitled *Childhood*.[32]

## III.

Throughout his work, Robert Walser was constantly concerned with a poetic of childhood across various fields of literary production, a poetic that, like Rilke, is embedded in the context of pedagogic debates and developmental psychology research around 1900.[33] The first prose publication—in 1904, entitled *Fritz Kocher's Essays*—is a collection of fictional texts by a schoolboy who died at a young age, discussing subjects of the most general kind like nature, man, friendship, fatherland, or school. With the mannered simplicity of a child, which contrasts curiously with his precocity, Walser indicates that his intention is not to realistically render the point of view of a middle school pupil; rather, the work is to be understood as a staging of naïvety.[34] The formal structure itself is already a part of this staging, with which Walser is doubtlessly exploring the contemporary call to capture and reflect the specific perceptions of a child. The construction of a first-person in-fantile narrator, still a novelty in the field of canonic literature around 1900, align *Fritz Kocher's Essays* to the progressive agenda, an agenda Walser was familiar with thanks to his personal contact with Ellen Key[35] and that expressly set the goal to consider the world through the eyes of children.

The staging of child subjectivity serves Walser as a means to relate his first novel to pedagogical questions significantly influenced by the educational controversies raging at the turn into the new century. The narrative allows a schoolboy to speak, and he duly refers constantly to the standardizing norms and conditions imposed by school education. Within the institution, to which the child seems to have an affirmative relationship, the position of the teacher is however subjected to blatant subversion at times, Walser depicting him in such a way that he displays, despite their vastly different statures, an unmistakable affinity to Saint Nicholas:

> The teacher sits at his desk like a hermit between high cliffs. [...] The teacher is a short, frail, feeble man. I've heard it said that men like that are the smartest and most learned. That may well be true. I am firmly convinced that this teacher is infinitely smart. I wouldn't want to bear the burden of his knowledge. [...] The teacher is very excitable. He often flies into a terrible rage when a schoolboy makes him angry by not being able to do something. That's wrong. Why get excited about something as minor as a schoolboy being lazy? [...] You need a very special kind of talent to be a teacher. To keep your dignity faced with rascals like us all day long requires a lot of willpower. All things considered our teacher has good self-control. [...] He is very properly dressed, and it's true that we laugh behind his back a lot. A back is always a little ridiculous. There's nothing you can do about it. He wears high boots, as though just returning from the Battle of Austerlitz.

These boots that are so grand, only the spurs are missing, give us a lot to think about. The boots are practically bigger than he is. When he is really mad, he stamps his feet with them. I'm not very happy with my portrait.[36]

One can take this teacher portrait to be a minor written rebellion against the authority represented by the institution of the school. With the hyperbolic soldier boots, their spurs recalling the strict schoolmasterly drilling and disciplining of the Wilhelmine period, military imagery is used to describe the atmosphere of a schoolroom. In Fritz Kocher's class however, this does not deter the children from ridiculing the teacher. Not only do they secretly laugh at him behind his back, he is described as being small and frail in stature, indeed almost smaller than his large boots, into which he even seems to disappear. And like Napoleon at Austerlitz, the teacher is the vanquished in the everyday school routine, for it makes him irritable and he quickly loses his temper, while the children remain quiet and calm. Analogous to the episode in *Struwwelpeter*, it is not the child who loses control but the master, who becomes furious and has to try and keep his composure. In Walser's scene, criticism of school is expressed through a caricature that counters the traditional image of the overpowering teacher in front of an intimidated class quivering with fear, while in its final sentence, almost as if in passing, attention is drawn to how the traditional classroom is not a place where well-crafted texts can be written. Nowhere is Walser's later remark more fitting: "there are authors who have placed letters like Struwwelpeter."[37]

Going by the turnabout in the final sentence of the portrait of the teacher, Walser's exploration of reformist positions extends to writing itself, which under the conditions of the institution is one of the main topics in *Fritz Kocher's Essays*. The boy also writes school essays about the school essay. This brings a text genre into focus that is a political issue around 1900, the subject of fierce and polemical debate. No less a figure than Wilhelm II personally announces his intention to "make German the basis" of schooling and the "German school essay must be the center that all else revolves around," because it is the only reliable standard for judging whether a pupil is "worth their salt or not."[38] Contrastingly, the anti-authoritarian movements work against the government's schooling plans, not only complaining that these would produce normalized subjects subservient to the state instead of creative individuals, but moreover directly launching their campaign where the state defines its very center of power in this context, namely the essay, which they now elevate to a means allowing children to freely express their imagination and individuality, an opportunity to display their creative resourcefulness and original, almost poetic ingenuity. Very much aware of the normative implications of this instrument of domination,[39] Fritz Kocher thus dares onto explosive terrain when he speaks about the choice to write what he wants:

> This time, the teacher said, each of you can write whatever comes to mind. To be honest, nothing comes to mind. I don't like this kind of freedom. I am happy to be tied to a set subject. I am too lazy to think of something myself. And what would it be? I'm equally happy to write about anything. I don't like hunting around for a topic, I like looking for beautiful, delicate words. I can come up with ten, even a hundred ideas from one idea, but the original idea never comes to me. What do I know. I write because it's nice to fill up the lines with pretty little letters like this. The "what" makes no difference to me at all.[40]

With these considerations, Fritz Kocher seems to be diametrically opposed to the progressive reformists, for the existence of a self-activating nature and a child possessing a lively
imagination are doubted, and thus with them the pedagogic
agenda itself. Fritz obviously has no inkling of what he should
do with the freedom given to him, preferring, as he concedes,
set topics. Unlike what the reformist educators wish to believe, in Walser there is nothing inherently genial to the child,
nothing intrinsically spontaneous and creative, and it is in
this sense that his texts lack the pathos informing the prose
of the reformers. And yet, this is not a contrary position to the
new doctrine of education. Walser is in fact echoing the initial
difficulties pupils encountered upon the introduction of the
new essay format.[41] Considered in this light, Fritz Kocher is
actually abiding by the norms of the open-topic essay, and in
fact does so with such devotion that the reformist demands
are met perfectly and completely: Walser's young protagonist
writes a text under the title of "open topic" and the essay is
then, quite literally, left open. Fritz Kocher's true freedom resides in taking the liberty to say nothing, and be open enough
to admit that the only thing he finds appealing about writing
is filling in the lines with delicate letters without any semantic content. Emerging with this freedom is an aspect of childhood that obstinately eludes educational intrusion and har-
bors the nucleus of a subversive force against the pedagogic
apparatus: infantile writing, as pure graphic, remains poised
on the surface, without the material letters penetrating to the
depth of meaning. At the threshold of representation, child
writing works along the exteriorities of language, precisely
where language is not yet communicative and its sensory con-
cretion has priority over signification.

It is this exteriority of language that continuously informs Robert Walser's poetic and more precisely determines the importance of infantility in his writings. The moralizing pedagogical discourse about "naughty children," who resist the adult world with their unreason, spontaneity, and creativity, is at best a makeshift means to understand Walser's young heroes.[42] Liberated from the prescribed rules of development, Walser's children inhabit a liminal realm hovering between language and non-language, and this side of familial and pedagogical regimens, or formulated more generally: the boyish protagonists like Fritz Kocher steadfastly persist before the symbolic realm and are characterized by a primordial intractability. They therefore cannot be reduced to a social explanatory model. In a prose piece entitled "The End of the World," Walser describes how they are fundamentally out of reach of controlling influences and parents: "A child who had neither father and mother nor brother and sister, was member of no family and utterly homeless, hit on the idea of running off, all the way to the end of the world."[43]

The theme of childhood pervades Walser's literary work as a figure of poetological reflection through to the late production—his writings are permeated by the infantile, evident not only in the omnipresent motifs of childhood, but also in how he works, ever more radically, with the materiality of language. From the period between 1924 and 1933, 526 small pieces of paper have survived which due to the miniscule writing on them, illegible to the naked eye, have become famous as the *Microscripts* and were first made accessible in text form after decades of painstaking deciphering.[44] Long mystified as the pinnacle of Walser's mysteriousness and seen in connection with his later "mental illness," the purported secret code turns out to be part of a well-organized writing method, whereby in most cases the micrographic pencil sketches are identifiable as preliminary stages of texts to be subsequently transcribed into clean copy and eventually published.[45] Upon closer examination, what at first glance looks like a block, and could justifiably be seen as scribbling, proves to be an extreme miniaturization of Walser's particular use of *Kurrent* script. Amongst the diverse attempts to explain this unorthodox practice is the assumption that the move into the miniscule reflects a "mimetic assimilation of children's play" and that Walser's "mischievous intent to camouflage" grew out of a "childlike naturalness."[46] This thesis misses what is played out in the texts when it relates Walser's impish childishness to a psychosocial idea of childhood and understands the ostensible "camouflaging magic of the microscript" as the literary self-assertion of a *puer aeternus*, eternally a child thanks to his creative spirit, against the demands of the world.[47] Walser's infantility springs rather from an emphatic negation of conceptions of ingenious creativity. In one of the few documents in which the author gave more or less veiled clues to the peculiarities of his minimalistic handwriting—the often-quoted letter to the editor Max Rychner of June 20 1927—the microscript is presented as a childlike practice and deliberately positioned on the threshold of writing. Following a crisis in his literary production, understood as arising from a physiological problem, a "real breakdown in my hand," Walser overcame the "period of disruption" with the help of a new writing technique. By beginning to "pencil-sketch, to scribble, to fiddle about," writing became play and this revived his enthusiasm. While writing these pencil micrograms he "learned again to write—like a little boy."[48] In his calculated use of the dash Walser marks the threshold that reveals micro-play to be the child's entrance into the realm of writing.[49]

Micrography is presented as an infantile realm prior to the symbolic order. Walser dwells in this realm in what will be his final decade of literary production in a very concrete material and technical sense. This pertains not only to his selection of writing instrument, recommended in the reform schools of the 1920s as the preferred means for learning to write, namely the pencil, or the length of the texts, which is oriented on the school essay;[50] it also entails the very physical practice of writing, which reactivates educational techniques when it combines learning to write with drawing and thus recalls a potent connection in the history of the didactics of writing and composition.[51] "Writing, authoring, seems to me to stem from drawing," notes Walser on microscript 93 in a self-reflective moment.[52] In its graphical form, Walser's microscript visualizes a zone of non-difference between writing and drawing that challenges the boundaries of readability in a way unprecedented in the literary tradition. Decades of laborious deciphering work was required to recognize that what was supposedly nothing but "scribble" are in fact language "signs." The path from grapheme to the meanings connected with letters and words—so we may conclude—can not only be long, but on the way it passes through an exteriority of the sign which, resistive to meaning, in Walser's micrographic pencil system is dissected into its very component parts.[53] The miniscule letters may appear to be a shrunken, depleted form when compared to fully-fledged normal writing and, consequently, repeatedly seen in connection with a heroically isolated literature of concealing and vanishing.[54] Far from possessing an antecedent and firmly-established unity (of the subject, the sign, the text), which can then be mischievously masked or destructed, the miniscule writing is by no means a manifestation of disintegration—it is rather a script that, principally readable, Walser used and professionalized over a number of years, the aesthetic appeal residing in how it, in a kind of archeology of the media, perpetuates the infantile learning and practicing of the very act of writing. In contrast to Rilke's elegiac gesture, Walser, with disarming matter-of-factness and the tacit radicalness of irony, presupposes that, at bottom, childhood can never be shed completely.

## IV.

The world of the child and the nature of childhood are amongst the most persistent subjects in the work of writer and critic Walter Benjamin. Although Benjamin never formulated a coherent theory, his constant reflection on these subjects is manifested in a diverse array of heterogeneous texts. After abandoning the Youth Movement (*Jugendbewegung*) and turning away from his teacher Gustav Wyneken, the first indications of Benjamin's interest in childhood emerge as early as the mid-1910s with sketches on the aesthetics of the imagination and colors.[55] Upon becoming a father in 1918, Benjamin begins to keep a notebook, documenting—until 1932—with evident fascination how his son Stefan acquired and used language throughout childhood.[56] Concurrently, he collects children's books, some 200 of which have been preserved.[57] From the mid-1920s, this dedication to the subject finds its expression in an imposing number of reviews and short treatises, which tangibly reveal how pivotal the various facets of this topic had become to Benjamin. The thematic range is vast: children's books[58] and contemporary reading primers,[59] through to the cultural history of toys[60] and proletarian children's theatre[61] and pedagogy in general.[62] In *One*

*Way Street* from 1928, there are altogether six *Denkbilder* ("thought-images") on the motif of the child, three of which had already been previously published in 1926 under the title of "Children" in an issue of the journal *Die literarische Welt* dedicated to children's literature.[63] At the end of the 1920s and the early 1930s, Benjamin then writes several radio stories for children which were produced and broadcast by the FunkStunde AG in Berlin and the Südwestdeutscher Rundfunk.[64] After his detailed study of the work of Marcel Proust, in the 1930s Benjamin's interest eventually focuses on the ongoing project of childhood memories, meanwhile famous as *A Berlin Chronicle*[65] and *Berlin Childhood around 1900*.[66] He worked on these texts until his death without finding a form suitable for a completed book.[67] It is in this context that Benjamin, in the "Doctrine of the Similar" and "On the Mimetic Faculty," also develops a theory of mimesis and language, the heart of which is an anthropological perspective on how children play.[68]

When searching for a stringent conception on childhood underpinning and connecting these varied writings, then at least two premises emerging out Benjamin's critical examination of the Youth Movement need emphasizing.[69] Firstly, Benjamin distances himself from its reformist education program, disputing its anthropological optimism. He emphatically continues the modern practice of demystifying the bourgeois myth of an idealized childhood, tacitly referring to the writings of Sigmund Freud when he underlines "the grotesque, cruel, grim side" in a child's life and contrasts this with the naïvety of those "meek and mild educators" who "still cling to Rousseauesque dreams."[70] While the latter assume that humans are innately good, and thus contend that it must be possible to bring up a child, the creature of nature *par excellence*, to be an extraordinarily pious, decent, and sociable person, Benjamin, casting an eye towards writers like Joachim Ringelnatz and painters like Paul Klee, points out the "despotic and dehumanized element in children."[71] Contrary to the claims of some commentators,[72] Benjamin refuses to join his contemporary progressive reformist educators in espousing a Romanticized idealization. Instead of glorifying the child as an innocent angel or a superior human being, he uses the term "dehumanized" to level a forthright criticism of the humanist foundations of the reform movement. Moreover, Benjamin reproaches contemporary pedagogy for its "infatuation with psychology."[73] As he sees it, any "psychological insight into the internal life of the child" is geared to serve the goals of an entertainment industry that has lost its "ethical content" and whose products foster a misguided idea of childhood.[74] Here Benjamin discerns a "colonizing logic" at work, one that is tantamount to commandeering the "tender and withdrawn imagination of the child" and recasting it as an "emotional demand in the interests of a commodity-producing society," thus turning it, as it were, into a "sales opportunity for cultural goods."[75] The purpose behind this scathing criticism is to realign the trajectory of interest in the child, to re-orientate it "not psychologically [...] but factually."[76] In a pivotal passage in *One Way Street* he observes:

> For children are particularly fond of haunting any site where things are being visibly worked on. They are irresistibly drawn by the detritus generated by building, gardening, housework, tailoring, or carpentry. In waste products they recognize the face that the world of things turns directly and solely to them. In using these things, they do not so much imitate the works of adults as bring together, in the artifact produced in play, materials of

> widely differing kinds in a new, intuitive relationship. Children thus produce their own small world within the greater one. The norms of this small world must be kept in mind.[77]

What Benjamin describes here is nothing less than the capacity of the child to turn to and delve in the underbelly of the instrumentally rationalized world of adults. Children do not accept the given meaning of things; by virtue of an unprejudiced sensual-haptic approach, they experience objects in a way while playing that unlocks new potential meanings. As the source from which the "revolutionary force"[78] of a candid cognition springs, Benjamin understands this to be a "nursery of profane epiphany" and a Messianic figure.[79] At the same time, the child's "small world" emerges as a marginal phenomenon, and thus has the potential to proffer the cultural analyst central insights into social relations and their obscured possibilities. This focus pertains not only to child play, which, parallel to the discourse of developmental psychology, attracts Benjamin's interest in the sense of an ethnography of his own culture;[80] it also involves fostering attention for the phenomenon of language acquisition, explored by Benjamin in a series of texts which shed light on how a child enters the world of writing and script. In a note from 1929 entitled "A writing child" for example, Benjamin describes learning to write:

> The writing hand is suspended in the scaffolding of the lines like an athlete in the giddy-making wall-bars of the arena (or of the theatre-flies). Mouse, hat, house, twig, bear, ice, and egg fill the arena—a pale, glacial audience. They watch their dangerous tricks.
>
> *Salto mortale* of the *s* / watch how the hand seeks the place on the page where it should make a start. The threshold before the

realm of writing. When the child writes, its hand sets off on a journey. A long journey with pauses for it to spend the night. The letter disintegrates into pauses. Panic and paralysis of the hand. The pain of leaving the accustomed landscape of space, because from now on it may move only along the surface.[81]

As the example of this note—written on small, lined note-paper and not published in his lifetime—shows, Benjamin's handwriting was also extremely small. Unaware of Walser's microscript, this "tendency towards microscopic handwriting"[82] needs to be considered in the context of a keen interest in the phenomenon of miniaturization, which Benjamin had already reflected on as the characteristic signum of children's play. Just as diminution can remove any object from the sphere of normal usage and turn it into a plaything, Benjamin's graphic miniatures place a pronounced emphasis on the tiny and the playful in an age in which all else seems to be remorselessly striving to be large and great.[83] Addressing the child's playful passage into the "realm of writing," Benjamin's act of writing enacts the scene of its own genesis. The entry into the orders of the symbolic is not only vividly described discursively but also visualized through the graphical materiality of writing.

The miniature threshold narrative illuminates a zone to be traversed in the passage that Benjamin reveals to be precipitous, akin to hovering over an abyss.[84] The space before writing is imagined as an arena in which there is nothing stable to hold onto, nor any clear orientation. Like a wordplay, the "hand" of the child "hangs suspended" in the lines of the paper, here writing exercises are done shakily in "giddy-making wall-bars," no words formed, but tottering from letter to letter, here is a site of anthropological and cultural liminality,[85] where no fixed and certain meanings exist. Attention is focused exclusively on the starting point of writing, on the very moment the pencil touches the paper and leaves behind the space of the pre-literate, and from then on moves solely on and across the surface: "watch how the hand seeks the place on the page where it should make a start." The note stages the entry into the symbolic as a *rite de passage*, ridden with anxiety and the fear of loss, ambiguities abounding and awaiting. The handwritten note itself, upon closer inspection, reveals the threshold to be an indefinite zone, its indefiniteness making it close to impossible to locate the passage. Reading the phrase, as the editors have, as the "threshold *before* the realm of writing" results from a conjectural intervention[86] that blurs the point the note is making, for the crossing-over does not follow the model of chronological linearity and thus mark an antecedent space prior to language clearly and distinctly from a subsequent space of language and writing; reading it in the manuscript version as the "threshold *of* the realm of writing," the note indicates rather that children's script is coexistent with writing as its unrecoverable but continually present origin. *Before* writing is always already part *of* writing (and reciprocally), or in other words: there is no cultural order grounded in itself that would not be touched and affected by this originary groundlessness, as conversely, there is not a pure and pretemporal sphere that is not already in a zone of the passage. Thus, the hand of the child at the beginning of the note, still before writing has been learned, is introduced as a "writing hand." The impossibility of discursively coming to grips with the realm prior to the symbolic is demonstrated by Benjamin in all its graphic-literal consequence.

The note aims at an experience adults cannot repeat (or recapture)[87]—how a child is on an uncertain path to language

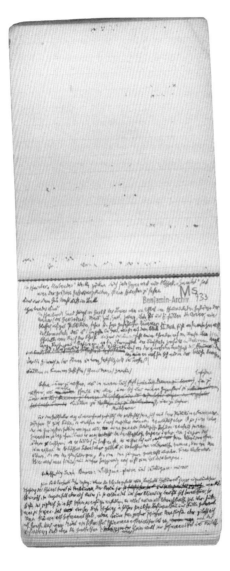

FIG. 5: Walter Benjamin, "A writing child" (manuscript, 1929).

from the very outset of life, with crossing over into writing the final and irreversible step to be taken. For Benjamin, in essence this experience, usually subsumed under the pedagogical verb "to learn," is incalculable, a view that emerges in his examination of contemporary writing didactics. Directly connected with "A writing child" are two reviews of play primers by Tom Seidmann-Freud, Sigmund Freud's niece (born Martha Gertrud Freud), who was one of the most important book illustrators of the Weimar Republic. Imbued with the spirit of the new pedagogics, Benjamin welcomes that these primers are underpinned by an idea of "learning" oriented on and appropriate for children—precisely because they set the learning process in motion by activating the play instinct. The primer, notes Benjamin

> [...] is not oriented towards "appropriation" and "mastery" of a particular task—this style of learning only suits grown-ups—, rather it takes account of the child, for whom learning, as with everything else, naturally signifies a great adventure.[88]

Learning to write in the primers should therefore proceed indirectly via drawing, painting, and scribbling, aiming to "develop a desire to write out of the joy in drawing."[89] As a pictographic script, letter writing steps forward in its original dual dynamic of readability and visibility—a generally obscured moment that is brought into sharp relief not only by Walser's but also Benjamin's micrographic practice. Perceived as a graphic formation, the miniature writing recalls those scribblings by a child which, according to Benjamin, defy censoring by some sort of "meaning" and wherein the words gather for a "masquerade."[90] A child's dealings with language and writing are characterized fundamentally by how these are yet to be communicative, that they—in an *in-fantile* sense—*say nothing*.

For all his affinity with the reformist education pro-gram—Benjamin noting in a critical diagnosis that its rise is due not to the "progress of science" but the "downfall of authority"[91]—, the works of Seidmann-Freud cannot hide the fact that entry into writing represents a moment pedagogy can never capture and at bottom cannot be taught. "Where children play a secret lies buried"[92] is Benjamin's formula for the impossibility to control this event. Upbringing is not pro-grammable and is in essence unpredictable—it is this peda-gogical imponderability that Benjamin also recognizes in the caricatures of *Struwwelpeter* and influenced him to become an enthusiastic advocate of this controversial children's book. In the review with the playful title *Springing Beginnings* ("Grünende Anfangsgründe", *Greening Shoots*) from 1930, Benjamin places the new primers close to *Struwwelpeter*, for in both works—despite the grave doubts about the pedagogy of the bad example—what is suited for children is found in the principle of exaggeration. Not without ambiguity, he calls exaggeration a "mighty hand" (*eine gewaltige Hand*) that lies protectively over children.[93] Surprisingly, a violence becomes discernible in the new primers as well, one that the playful may distract from, but is still present nonetheless as a protective force, for the children encounter it when they learn to write: this is the "horror with which the first letters so willingly form as idols in front of the child."[94] Lying in wait at the threshold of writing, this horror emanates from the "spell of the black-on-white, from law and order, the irrevocable, of their essence being determined for eternity."[95] At the threshold of writing, a potential violence of the symbolic becomes discernible that, while lying beyond the disciplinary coercion imposed by the old pedagogy and its flogging methods, the new educational sciences are also incapable of preventing. It is in this analytical sense that we can understand how in an early text on school reform Benjamin came to the utterly non-utopian view that upbringing "will never be resolvable without violence."[96] What begins to emerge in Benjamin's reviews of the primers is how the play with letters, which he so virtuously interwove into his childhood memories in *Berlin Childhood around 1900* and, moreover, in a material sense, elevated to the standard for his micrographic writing, is not tied to the promise of reconquering a paradisiacal origin, but can only be partaken in by paying the price of a "miserable rightlessness."[97] The passage into the realm of the symbolic is irreversible—once having learnt to write and begun to communicate using letters and words there is no return.[98] As with Rilke and Walser, there is simply no other conclusion to reach for Benjamin.

Childhood therefore remains only present as "unforgettable"[99]—it can neither be forgotten but nor can it ever be completely restored by being remembered; it stands for "all the individual or collective life that is forgotten with each instant."[100] In this negative form of remembering what is lost, childhood points to the shaky ground on which the trusted orders stand, without which, as Benjamin sees it, no new possibilities of existence are conceivable.

## V.

In connection with the emerging child and developmental psychology, which since the 1850s had set about "to discern and to decipher the mysterious writing on the mind of the child,"[101] new positions in the context of the educational sciences are established around 1900; gathered under the name reform pedagogics, they strive to comprehend the "real nature of children."[102] The literature of Modernism joins this—discourse-defining at the turn of the century—project, drawing from it various conclusions for literary practice. While Rilke, influenced by a perceived original loss of the voice, practices an elegiac writing, the scriptoral gesture gains even greater importance in Walser and Benjamin. Considering the pre-history of writing, the micrographic practices of Walser and Benjamin, due to their notational iconicity, are closely affiliated to scribbling—they are to be considered in the context of a "de-differentiation of writing and drawing"[103] and with this recall the childhood experiences of acquiring writing skills, the concern not only of school didactics but also concurrently attracting the interest of experimental psychologists like James Baldwin, James Sully, and others. In Rilke, Walser, and Benjamin, it becomes clear that the inky children inherently possess a genuine resistance towards the symbolic. Beyond the educational coercion, they retain something of their mute and untamable strangeness. The focus of attention is neither on a state of deficiency, which needs to be rectified and overcome through education, nor a preliminary stage to becoming a human being that needs to be retrieved; rather, an anonymous being untouched by prescriptive development, with whom all ascriptions adults seek to impose are condemned to failure. With this figure the literary texts of Modernism mark a literal *in-fantility*, one that is to be overcome and halted by the conventional "education to maturity," programmatic since the Enlightenment, mobilizing all available means, but that now comes to prominence as a poetological metaphor of production and is rendered visible in the form of dashes (Rilke) and graphic play (Walser, Benjamin).

Literature around 1900 approaches the *infans* on the threshold to language and writing, reflecting the difficulties encountered and the resistance provoked, the abysses and uncertainties, but also the original openness of meaning and the myriad possibilities when symbolic formations arise.[104] As the German psychologist and linguist Karl Bühler, whose language theory published in 1918 is based on experimental research into child scribbling and babbling, put it, "human culture has not fallen from heaven readymade, but like all else that is alive and animate it has arisen gradually."[105] In contrast to what the concurrently burgeoning discipline of structural linguistics claims,[106] there is no language without childhood.

# Becoming-Child (*Walser*)

## I.

Robert Walser's children are unformed "somethings" who, while generally called a "child," in every respect remain indeterminate.[1] There is a small hiatus between naming and the named, one that Walser marks incisively at a significant place in his *Microscripts* in the form of a *contradictio in adjecto*, stating "that a child is somehow a determinacy."[2] The irritating characteristic of Walser's children resides in how they only reveal themselves to a degree before once again eluding every effort to exercise authority and control over them. They frequently appear in passing and stay anonymous, as if following an innate desire to hide. They are thus called a variety of names, "lad," "rascal," "scoundrel," "lout," "barbarian," "nipper," "kiddy," "peewee," or quite simply "the child." Like these other names, the generic designation "child" is an antonomasia for something small, wild, and nameless—for a something that blocks itself off from all the fixating constraints of familial or pedagogic definitions. At heart, all of Walser's texts are stories about children. They are grounded in a continuous poetic fascination with the child and infantile figures, habituating a zone of radical intractability: "It is absolutely only itself, otherwise seemingly nothing else."[3] Each and every attempt to reveal the hidden kernel of a child is repulsed.[4] If we take the turn to this being to be the creative trajectory of Walser's writing, then the focus needs to be placed on plotting a movement that does not follow a myth, a profound mystery, or an archetype. Rather, *becoming-child* means for Walser a devotedly attentive adaptation of the undetermined—of a state un-marked, of emptiness, of a-significance.


## II.

A microscript draft published under the title *Der Schlingel* (*The Rascal*) tells of a child who may be read as the poetological emblem of Walser's writing:

> Fortunately while willing to form the abstract, the lid to a crate interrupts me, which a boy, a really stupid lad, who had care-fully nested himself in the crate, which could just as easily be a suitcase, snaps shut to revel in the joy of hiding, exclusively an enjoyment for boys adults can only understand by surmounting enormous difficulties, i.e. with great effort. This takes place in an attic where bedsteads, rods, basins, presses, baskets of all types, the useful and the thrown-out-of-use, are kept. [...] Teeming as it is here with crates, boys, women, and letter envelopes, in which letters lie, then it is quite right to speak of a clutter. And it is only understandable that the mother of the lout choosing the crate as his place of residence started to look for him eagerly once she began to miss his presence. [...] Mother most certainly looked beautiful as she said to herself: "He causes me such worry. It's so naughty of him." At the same time, the certainty that he is mak-ing fun of her took up more and more space in her upper story, which looks as noble, i.e. as gracious as it is beautiful and serene, whereby the author means her forehead, across whose surface scarcely noticeable tiny creases run like wavelets from time to time. [...] Nevertheless, the darkness, which he saw himself in a position to enjoy to the full in all its details, had become too interesting that he could have fancied slipping out of it, for he

must have been inclined to consider it enthralling in itself. [...] The lad in the crate had mounted a victorious conquest by taking possession of the crate, he was now no longer just what he otherwise was, but someone who had become precious because one was now fearful for his sake. Bit by bit he enjoyed this pleasantly tingling importance, beholding it after all as an overbrightness, which preserved the intelligence he required to characterize himself, with more or less definiteness, as a barbarian. Did he know that, in a certain sense, barbarians, i.e. ingenuous natures are distinct from self-conscious cultural ones laden full with thoughts large and small? Perhaps he felt, sensed it more than he knew it. [...] Several times the wildling [...] had begun to lift the lid a little with cute caution, but then retreated back into the enclosededness, which had begun to make him impatient [...]. Barbarians love, in some measure, the smell, the pomp, the sound of dangers. Perhaps they are less conscious of this than the intellectually branched, the existence dissectors, the shredded souls, the fully splintered, the differentiated who know it all the more. The barbarians or lads presumably don't know the adults or the civilized as well as they know them, which, by the way, does not necessarily correspond to the precision of exact observation.[5]

Seemingly meandering, if not laborious, the narrative tells of a boy who finds great joy in hiding from his mother. He burrows into the darkness of a crate in the attic, where things "useful and the thrown-out-of-use" are stored, and thus where the logic of normal usage is reversed and invalidated. A "Gnush" reigns in this child heterotopia *par excellence*, a Swiss German expression for "mess, disorder, confusion"—or in short: a "clutter"—that from the very outset is the thematic center of the microscript sketch. The disarray thus refers not only to all the things in the attic, but also the household order, which falls apart when the child evades maternal control by creating his own realm and enters into a self-relationship when facing the darkness *en détail.* The prose piece ends with the mother, much to her relief, eventually finding the child and giving him—in a *mise en abyme*—a "benign reproach" and simultaneously provides the author with the title: "the rascal."[6] Like the young boy who finds the place proper to him in a crate amidst but apart from the prevailing circumstances, Walser had preserved the products—or so to speak: the "children"— of his micrographic writing in a shoebox, holding them back to the very end from the world with all its claims and demands. And as this literary practice evades conventional ascriptions, the misbehaving young boy also demonstrates his elusiveness, his nature defying any certain definition. In its concrete form, the story of the young rascal is readable as a parable for Walser's graphical method and practice, which is oriented on the logic of children's play and thus fails to find a firm place in the prevailing order of the adults, whereby conversely they can only ever understand infantile activities by mustering the effort to "surmount enormous difficulties" because they lack an appreciation of the logic inherent to the child. As the prose piece *Mutter und Kind* (*Mother and Child*) from 1929, based on the microscript sketch, makes clear, the enormous innovative poetical potential of Walser's writing resides in the effort to "enter into and immerse in what the child is doing."[7]

The focus on the rascal in the dark crate indicates that Walser definitely has the contemporary discourse on childhood in mind, specifically where this discourse is strongly characterized by ethnological notions of the primitive.[8] Just as development psychologists around 1900 aid an estrangement of the child so that—analogous to the savage—it is excluded from the realm of civilization, Walser takes up this sharply-drawn contrast between adults and children when examining the gap between the generations in the imagery of the barbarians and the civilized. On the face of it, he is following the cultural-critical model in the Rousseauian-Romantic tradition that enjoyed enormous popularity amongst the reformist pedagogical movements of the time and propagated a markedly positive reevaluation of the child's mode of existence. Whereas the child emerges as a primordial and naïve natural being, at one with itself, adults are afflicted by the wounds of reflection. Accordingly, they are described in the text as "the intellectually branched, the existence dissectors, the shredded souls, the fully splintered, the differentiated." Equally, the uninhibited natures stand out from the "self-conscious cultural ones laden full with thoughts large and small," as if the world of the child, home to a non-alienated and naïve existence, were on a higher plane. This model can only pertain to a certain extent however, and here Walser subtly casts doubt on it, querying two aspects. Firstly, upon closer inspection the divide does not run between children and adults but rather through the child itself, for in the text it is not the narrator but the rascal who, sitting in the dark crate, calls himself a barbarian, creating a reflective distance to himself; secondly, the difference between children and adults is intensified as an epistemic problem, for the suspicion is expressed that neither side can really know anything about the other. In line with this ignorance, a persistent indeterminacy inheres to the discourse on the child in Walser's work, an indeterminacy that is evident from the very outset. The child is without substance, it is solely definable as the diffuse other of its own culture who is scarcely intelligible for adults. Contrary to the pedagogic programs which, in the footsteps of Rousseau, had turned the child into an arena for all manner of idealizations and disciplining measures, and, now also joined by reformist pedagogy around 1900, understood it as an educable being in small format—but despite everything still as *human*—, something emerges in the figure of the barbarian that Walter Benjamin had identified as the "dehumanized in children."[9] It is thus clear that Walser is also questioning nothing less than the humanist tenet of the child's human resemblance.

## III.

The uncertainty enshrouding how to classify the child is still very much an issue around 1900. Grimm's *Dictionary*, an inexhaustible source for understanding language and thought at the turn of the century, contains the following entry: "Child, n. pl. children, *proles*, *infans*, *liberi*; the neuter is used to cover both sexes (cf. human), or rather to characterize the sex as still of no importance, as not yet existent, as with lamb, calf, fawn, pets."[10] Considered from this attempt at a definition, the child is then to be viewed as a zone of total non-difference. All conventional distinctions are "not yet existent" and therefore inadequate—a child cannot be determined as female or male, nor clearly classed as human or animal. As an indefinite being, antecedent to all cultural markings, it features in one of Walser's microscript sketches entitled *I old calf ballbabbled with a kid*.

The text revolves around the encounter between an adult, who remains indistinct, and an anonymous child, who does not seem to belong to anyone and does nothing but play with a

Fig. 6: Robert Walser, *Microscript Sheet* 480r (1925).

ball. Their interaction is not only characterized by a significant inversion of the pedagogic situation, whereby this is fully in accord with the ideas put forward by reformist pedagogues, the adult supposed to learn from the child and not the other way around; moreover, their playing together intensifies into a dynamic that dissolves boundaries, eradicating all differences and opening up a fully empty space without any determinative fixations. Here, Walser is depicting nothing less than his literary program of *becoming-child*.

I old calf ballbabbeled with a kid. "Will you let me babble ball with you?" This was roughly my question. The dear kiddy's approval of my kiddishness made me so happy! But doesn't such happiness stamp one as a calf? Who dares to answer this question? I learned a lot from the child, I'm now excellent at babbling the ball. It's part patting, part throwing, sometimes dropping. I received the desirable explanation from the child and expressed my thanks in every respect by joyously keeping on kidding. To me it seemed apt to crawl from time to time. Crawl and along with it to be in an awfully good mood is firmly part of playing with a small child. [...] An undeniable cheerfulness resides in practicing. While I was fully immersed in the best and most eager kid- and calf-balling, the Russian student came and stood at the doorstep and gauged all my doings with a bewildered eye. She was speechless, and indeed what could she say to such outlandish calving? Perhaps, she thought that I was quite nice in the calf role. God, one can never know after all. Silently she withdrew to her studio or study. For mine, I thought: inside she devotes herself fully to efforts of the mind, whilst here in the merriment-filled hallway I'm lazily playing the calf. The student left the next day, and I'm writing these lines to remind her, she having taken with her a calving impression of me on holidays, what I'm cheeky enough not even to regret in the slightest, for she saw me in the purest happiness. How she appeared to me on the doorframe! A kidding calf must make a big impression on a Russian student. I'll yearn for her, I'll wish that she sees me babbleballing with the kid again. She was lovely in her student superiority, but the calf forbids any yearning. The calf has a lot to do, it demands something of itself, it looks with disdain at its kidding around.[11]

Positioned at the entrance to the sketch is a nameless "I" who describes himself as an "old calf" and is, one would like to assume, not an animal but an adult with a child's spirit. Although, when read literally, emulating infantile play may seem to be a foray into a realm beyond the human, the old calf demonstrates the human ability to learn something from the child, namely a practice described as "bällelen" ("playing ball"). This strange if not exotic word directly connects tonally into "old calf" ("Kalb") and determines the logic of production at work: as the child plays with the ball, so the text plays with language, echoing the words thrown up at the beginning according to the principle of onomatopoeia. The wordplay in the opening sentence points the way for the variations of the word to follow: "calf-balling," "calving," "calf role," "calving impression," through to "kidding calf." These structure the progression of the draft and mimic the word in its proverbial meaning: "the calf is, due to its playful and yet awkward leaps, in delight; of a human being who is still green, in whom infant exuberance is still too strongly present, particularly in an ungainly way, one says: he is still a calf."[12] Like a calf, the text itself is the product of a playful delight in writing, with the word "calf" thrown back and forth as when playing with a ball. Similarly, the Swiss German verb "bällelen" is to be read as a periphrasis for the generation of the text itself, which, as is stated in the sketch, is adapted from a genuinely childlike skill.

This literary mimicry of children's play brings into focus an aesthetic activity that is not only autonomous in its purposelessness—like the arts in terms of its classical definition. In Walser, one is only "wholly Man"[13] when they become visible in their substantial emptiness. A human finds their real determination in the silent play of the child only insofar as they become aware of their genuine indeterminacy. *Becoming-child* in Walser is the attempt to eradicate the boundary between adults and their other and to enter into a sphere of pure play, one in which the subject *radically gambles* and *ventures* to give themselves over to their primordial muteness. Consequentially, at the end of the text, the first-person I vanishes as the grammatical subject: "The calf has a lot to do, it demands something of itself," signaling the switch into the third person. Emerging from the encounter is an I-less calf that shares the state of I-lessness with the child. What adults only ever achieve with great effort is easy for children, for they are not bound to any fixed roles and can adopt new identities at will, as if they are indeed first with and in themselves when they are perpetually metamorphosing and eluding grasping in moments of being-out-of-oneself. Beyond the Romanticizing of an original state, the wish to become a child addresses a space that in kernel is meaningless, or *non-saying* in the sense of *in-fantile*, and wherein a nameless something moves around, with all those ascriptions mobilized by adults shattering against it, and in such a way that their perspective with its improvised concepts proves utterly deficient. For a child, *playing* is namely not an idle pastime, but—possibly— a deadly serious undertaking, often demanding the fierce tenacity of an animal.

FIG. 7: *Franz Kafka, approx. 5 years old* (1888).

# Little Hans (*Freud—Kafka*)

In his analysis of the formation of disciplinary society in *Discipline and Punish*, Michel Foucault identifies a new kind of interest in the human in the Modern Age. The social narrative no longer revolves around a hero whose adventures serve the purpose of providing a moral example. As Foucault elaborates, the individual now attracts attention because of a significant deviation from a norm. One effect of this shift is the proliferation of the case history. From the mid-eighteenth century it supplants the premodern genre of the *exemplum* and extends its reach beyond the boundaries of the human sciences.[1] While the *exemplum* tells the story of an individual regarded as exceptional solely for the fact that they stand out from the mass due to particularly exemplary behavior or conduct, the case history gives an account of the vita of a person who is an exception to the rule because they have strayed from the accepted norm. Accordingly, the protagonists of case histories are not ordinary citizens but criminals, maniacs, the ill, the perverse, etc. Foucault encapsulates this turnaround from the old *exemplum* to the modern case history thus:

> And if from the early Middle Ages to the present day the "adventure" is an account of individuality, the passage from the epic to the novel, from the noble deed to the secret singularity, from long exiles to the internal search for childhood, from combats to phantasies, it is also inscribed in the formation of a disciplinary society. The adventure of our childhood no longer finds expression in "*le bon petit Henri*", but in the misfortunes of "little Hans."[2]

Unlike the figure of *petit Henri*, who as the folk song relates ventures out into the wide world to eventually return to the safe coziness of home as a mature adult, Little Hans is cited as an example of the case of the modern human, i.e. for what an unexampled story of misfortune holds in store.

The following considerations put this thesis to the test and take a close look at the historical case of Little Hans. I will interrelate three texts which not only share the name Hans, but are also linked in terms of how they move within the tension, typical for the genre of case histories, between the particular and general: firstly, Sigmund Freud's *Analysis of a Phobia in a Five-Year-Old Boy* published in 1909, which became famous thanks to its subtitle of *Little Hans*; and secondly, two hand-written texts from Franz Kafka's literary remains in which a boy of the same name is the protagonist, revealing still undiscovered traces of Freud's case. Incisively, these stories join together in a complex entwinement between *casus* and *lapsus*, and are to be read as case histories in the double sense of the German *Fallgeschichte*. They refer, on the one hand, to the empirical *casus* of a child who became ill in 1905, a case that however proves extremely difficult to explain because of the elusiveness of the object of observation; on the other hand, the case histories of Freud and Kafka need to be read in the literal sense of relating a fall. Both draw on the example of Little Hans to narrate the story of childhood as that of a fall, a fall that determines the narrative motifs of the texts throughout and reveals a decidedly modern and unadorned conception of infantility. In both, the individual case serves as the medium through which a general history of childhood is examined and told, and not only the story of a unique life.

In Freud and Kafka however, the name Hans is not just understandable as a designation signaling the cumbersome anonymity of childhood; rather, the name also signalizes how, pivotal for modern case histories but differently weighted by both authors, the specific fact of individuality is unfathomable and the history of the individual case revolves around something that is mysterious and enigmatic. This complication becomes all the more evident as soon as one bears in mind an onomastic peculiarity: Hans is a common name, but at the same time Hans is a special name. This is the conclusion to be drawn when we consider *Grimm's Dictionary*, which notes the following under the respective lemma:

> [...] the frequent occurrence of the name leads to the conclusion that the same [...] goes beyond the narrower circle of a *nomen proprium* and is regarded as a salutation, a call, a name for male persons, whose specific names one does not know or will not use, so that one thus uses a name fitting several persons and, as it were, portrays more the general.[3]

The note explains the name's frequent occurrence with how Hans is also then used when the *nomen proprium* of an individual is passed over or simply unknown. In other words: every man can be called Hans. This is what is meant by "portraying more the general," but this tendency is only then really understood when we keep in mind that the special remains incognito. The name Hans is particular because it, like no other, is capable of naming what is not particular. When a case relates the fate of a Hans, then the individual only comes into focus to represent the general. As will become clear in the texts of Freud and Kafka, Hans is the paradigmatic name for the blind spots in every case history, blind spots which trigger a specific narrative dynamic innate to the genre.

## I.

In his meticulous rereading of Freud, Jacques Lacan assumes that the prime issue in the *Analysis of a Phobia in a Five-Year-Old Boy* is the phallus.[4] While it is indisputable that the interest circling around the "widdler" plays an important role for infantile sexuality, the concern plaguing the physician during the first ever psychoanalytical treatment of a child is another: Freud's text begins by noting that the case of the "very youthful patient" is characterized by methodological peculiarities.[5] Approaching Hans essentially as a subject who "knows how to speak,"[6] Lacan sees no fundamental difference to analyzing adults; Freud, however, expressly reflects on the limits of the classical talking cure in relation to the child. The difficulties stem from how the two most important techniques in analysis—free association and dream interpretation—are oriented on the logic of translating experience into language. Thus, as a rule, psychoanalysis requires patients who, as therapy unfolds, can verbalize repressed desires and conflicts. Because this requirement is not always unreservedly met by children, the talking cure threatens to come to nothing.[7] For many years, Freud had therefore been urging "my pupils and my friends to collect observations of the sexual life of children—the existence of which has as a rule been cleverly overlooked or deliberately denied."[8] The amount of material passed on to the master is not known—nevertheless one may contend that the case of little Hans was not randomly chosen. In this one case namely, Freud sees the imponderable nature of the

information gathered as counteracted by the first-order observer being invested with the authority of the physician and
the father:

> No one else, in my opinion, could possibly have prevailed on the
> child to make any such avowals; the special knowledge by means
> of which he was able to interpret the remarks by his five-year-old
> son was indispensable, and without it the technical difficulties
> in the way of conducting a psycho-analysis upon so young a child
> would have been insuperable. It was only because the author-
> ity of a father and of a physician were united in a single person,
> and because in him both affectionate care and scientific interest
> were combined, that it was possible in this one instance to apply
> the method to a use to which it would not otherwise have lent
> itself. [9]

Except for a single session where Freud directly takes part in
the treatment, it is the father of the boy who, under the su-
pervision of the teacher, conducts the analysis and takes the
notes. From the position of a second-order observer, Freud re-
stricts his role to selecting the notes for publication, arrang-
ing them to delineate how the case developed, and providing
critical comments. This reservation reveals not only methodological qualms, which may also be the reason why no other
analysis of a child by Freud is known; moreover, the unique
constellation is emphasized, the therapist underlining that
with little Hans he is relating an exceptional case defying gen-
eralization. Only this once did the method of the talking cure,
utterly unsuitable for treating children, prove effective—and
indeed the treatment ends with successful recovery.[10] In
terms of methodology, the following point is more decisive
however: firstly, with his introductory remark, Freud draws

attention to the complications which remain definitive for the history of child analysis in the twentieth century and subsequently lead to the development of new techniques by Anna Freud and Melanie Klein for example; secondly, Freud shakes off his doubts almost immediately and they play no further role in the case history. This step is not devoid of consistency however, for it is only at the cost of casting aside the aporiae of the method that the unique case of little Hans can be claimed to possess exemplary validity. In other words: the *casus stands and falls* on the assumption that the child's remarks can be unreservedly taken to be "avowals."

In this sense there can be no doubt that Freud publishes the study to furnish graphic evidence supporting the theses on infantile sexuality presented in the *Three Essays on the Theory of Sexuality* from 1905. The case history tells of an individual whose illness and its progression are reconstructed with the goal of becoming scientifically generalizable. One detail reveals that Freud was ready to openly disclose this strategy. The case is first mentioned in 1907 in a publication on the issue of sexual education for children and the child is still named "little Herbert."[11] And indeed, the analysis was of a boy called Herbert, namely Herbert Graf, the son of a musicology professor at the Vienna Academy, Max Graf. The erasing of the historical detail deliberately sets the case up to be shifted from a singular example to being "typical of the sexual development of children in general."[12] In view of the theory of prepubescent sexuality, oedipal structures, and the neurotic disorders entwined with them, Freud even comes to the conclusion at the end of his study that he has, strictly speaking, not learned anything new that he could have already surmised from treating adult patients.[13] Statements like these draw attention to a recursive structure of the text, for the case by no means serves to prepare knowledge that is to be first gained with the aid of empirical observation—rather, the empirical observation is steered by a kind of fore-knowledge that seeks confirmation for the respective hypotheses. Freud, who, as the regimen of scientific observation prescribes since time immemorial,[14] precisely notes the technical conditions of the procedure, makes no secret of the fact that the epistemic loop weakens the cogency of the case. At the same time, the text highlights that this difficulty is unavoidable and psychoanalysis is accordingly not to be understood as an unbiased examination but a therapeutic intervention. Thus, what from the practical side appears compelling, is theoretically an impasse: it is mentioned that much had to be suggested and indeed "told" to the child that he himself could not have said.[15] When Freud finally draws the conclusion that Hans is "really [...] a little Oedipus,"[16] then this statement does not go beyond the status of an intuitive hypothesis. It is one of the pitfalls of the case that the observed object comes straight to the point. After visiting Dr. Freud, Hans asks his father: "Does the Professor talk to God [...] as he can tell all that beforehand?"[17]

It is only with significant reservations that Freud's story of little Hans can be considered a representative individual case of infantile sexuality. Nor is its peculiarity limited to demonstrating the limits of such a generalizability. Rather, the text is characterized by how, in the form of noted exchanges, a particular material finds its expression. Set in a different typography to the analytical comments given by the adults, this material stands out because the boy's utterances are in various respects shaped by a narrative of falling. Three significant moments point to this.

Firstly, Freud adopts a perspective that draws on the philosophy of history. With the formation of the bourgeois subject in the second half of the eighteenth century, and more intensively since the conceptions of Romanticism, childhood was consistently idealized as a human paradise. Following Freud's insights, not much remains of the image of an angel-like natural being however. After diagnosing an astonishing agility in object choice and a polygamist disposition, combined with a pronounced homo- and auto-eroticism, Freud seems to get carried away and is moved to make the remarkable exclamation: "Little Hans seems to be a positive paragon of all the vices."[18] This exclamation, which varies the formulation of the "polymorphously perverse" child in the *Three Essays*,[19] not only marks an anthropological fall into the depths of sexuality. If children are to be seen as the paradisiac origin of humans, then Freud's depiction represents the fall of mankind, and so, a kind of original sin in the history of modern conceptions of childhood.

Secondly, the case possesses a nosologic peculiarity, for the case history is concentrated around the symptom of a marked phobia of falling things. Ever since observing a horse that fell while pulling a heavy wagon, the child fears stepping out onto the street. The father notes the following exchange:

> In the afternoon we again went out in front of the street door, and when I returned I asked Hans: "Which horses are you actually most afraid of?"
> Hans: "All of them."
> I: "That's not true."
> Hans: "I'm most afraid of horses with a thing on their mouths."
> I: "What do you mean? The piece of iron they have in their mouths?"

Hans: "No. They have something black on their mouths." (He covered his mouth with his hand.)

I: "What? A moustache, perhaps?"

Hans (laughing): "Oh no!"

I: "Have they all got it?"

Hans: "No, only a few of them."

I: "What is it that they've got on their mouths?"

Hans: "A black thing." (I think in reality it must be the thick piece of harness that dray-horses wear over their noses.) "And I'm most afraid of furniture-vans, too."

I: "Why?"

Hans: "I think when furniture-horses are dragging a heavy van they'll fall down."

[...]

I: "Why? Because it's so big?"

Hans: "No. Because once a horse in a bus fell down."

[...]

I: "What did you think when the horse fell down?"

Hans: "Now it will always be like this. All horses in buses'll fall down."[20]

A follower of Freud, the father is preoccupied with the expected idea that the phobia is actually related to the phallus, not least because Hans is avidly interested in the genitals of animals. But as the story soon makes clear, the fear is fixated on the movement of falling and not a specific object. Hans recoils not only at the falling van or the horse, but also from dropping feces or at the thought of "falling" into the bathtub.[21] If we take what he says seriously—that "now it will always be like this"—, then the inevitable conclusion is that for the boy the world is everything that falls. The step over the door sill—when interpreted with Lacan as the passage from the Imaginary to the Symbolic—means all that which has formed the foundations of his world is now called into question, shaky and uncertain.[22] One could accordingly assume that childhood is to be thought of as hesitating to grow up, as a wishing to remain under motherly care and shielding protection. But this is in fact not the case with Freud.

And why this is not the case leads to the third point—that a mythical importance is attached to the fall in the story of little Hans. In the conversation with his father, the boy is enticed to think that he could have associated defecating to giving birth. The father expands on this association:

> I: "When you sat on the chamber and a lumf came, did you think to yourself you were having a baby?"
> Hans (laughing): "Yes. Even at—Street, and here as well."
> I: "You know when the bus-horses fell down? The bus looked a like a baby-box, and when the black horse fell down it was just like..."
> Hans (taking me up): "...like having a baby."[23]

What emerges here is a story, recurrent in Freud, about human origins.[24] Like every myth, this narrative revolves around a deeply disconcerting kernel. If birth is understood as a movement of falling, in Freud's text childhood can be nothing other than a perpetual plummeting—a descent into a world which from the very beginning fails to offer any firm purchase and security. By reading Freud's depiction of a fall as a modern story of childhood, an infantile dread gains contours, one that could be justifiably called an existential *horror lapsus* and hence cannot be exhaustively comprehended with a reference to the triangulations of the bourgeois family.

## II.

The section planned as the thirteenth chapter of Franz Kafka's *The Castle*, which would turn out to be the author's final project, bears the simple title "Hans."[25] The protagonist is a young boy who appears once and then remains absent from the rest of the plot. Significantly, we are not told much about Hans. He is the son of the master shoemaker Otto Brunswick and in the fourth grade. He has stolen away from the classroom, hurrying off to help the land surveyor who has been degraded to the position of school janitor. The day before, K. and his fiancée Frieda have moved into the schoolhouse and are staying in one of the adjacent classrooms. In his futile struggle to gain the recognition of the castle authorities K. has hit a low point—earlier that morning the teacher has humiliated him in front of the assembled schoolchildren. Knocking on the door and entering, Hans stumbles however into a peculiar situation. He becomes entangled in a conversation that from the outset takes on forms typical of an interrogation. This fact deserves to be highlighted all the more because the surveyor had attracted much attention through his resolute opposition to the practices of the castle administration. With his "aversion to all manner of interrogations," K. appears to be willing to challenge the totalitarian claims the institution makes of the subject.[26] Nevertheless, he is now more than willing to ensnare the boy in a communicative situation that is subtly coercive. Although not in an institutional setting in the narrower sense, the conversation with Hans takes place in a classroom, and so the institution is never left. Following a topographical law of power, the surveyor adopts the role of the teacher, placing himself at the teacher's lectern while the boy sits at a desk and is exhorted to tell the truth. As the conversation unfolds, it becomes clear that K.'s questions are intended to extract "confessions" from the boy about his family life, for the land surveyor hopes to gain admittance to the castle through the boy's mother.[27] Frieda, present throughout, will later expose this strategy and use it as an opportunity to distance herself from her fiancé. In no uncertain terms she reproaches K. with having "mistreated" the boy[28]—a claim the land surveyor cannot deny.

We should not lose sight of the fact that the rigorous questioning reveals the impossibility of extracting a coherent family story from Hans. Because the boy only hesitatingly answers the questions or indeed not all, the following remark is given in the text:

> And now he had to speak about his mother, but he did so only hesitantly, after repeated requests, it became clear, though, that he was indeed a young boy, from whom, especially when he was asking questions, there seemed to issue a voice, perhaps in a premonition of the future, but perhaps this was merely a sensory illusion on the part of the uneasy tense listener, the voice of an almost energetic, clever man with foresight, but then without transition he was once again a schoolboy who was incapable of understanding certain questions and misinterpreted others and spoke too softly, with a childish inconsiderateness, even though this failing was repeatedly pointed out to him, and then, faced with some especially penetrating questions, he fell quite silent, as though out of stubbornness, and also without the slightest embarrassment, in a way no adult could have done.[29]

The difficulty in gaining information stems from how Hans is not an adult and does not abide by the usual rules of communication—the problem is thus not related to the nature of the specific individual but is methodological. Hans the child still embodies the Latin etymology, quite literally he is an *in-fans*, i. e. "non-saying." Whereas an interrogative situation is set up to get the subject to talk, this aim is doomed to fail in the case of children because their privilege, to not understand the question or to remain silent, inevitably entails the frustrating aborting of the questioning—and this is exactly what happens in the scene:

> Asked whether he had ever been at the castle, he answered only after repeated questioning, and what's more with a "No"; when asked the same question concerning his mother he simply did not answer. K. finally wearied of this, the questioning seemed useless even to him, for in that respect he agreed with the boy, there was also something rather shameful about this effort to probe family secrets in a roundabout way through an innocent child, and indeed doubly so if you couldn't even come up with anything.[30]

This passage emphasizes that Kafka's story of the boy Hans is an original case variation on little Hans. Here, the very same lacuna is placed in the foreground that Freud highlighted as an operative problem of child analysis, but then pushed aside as the case study continued.

An obvious objection to establishing such a connection to the *Analysis* is how it makes much of mere allusions. But this qualm is easily removed by recognizing that allusion is a pivotal structural feature of Kafka's literary signification process. Along with the boy's name, a whole series of further clues justifies linking the two texts. The following are just some of the most important. Although the details given are sparse, it is clear that the familial relations in which Hans is growing up are structured on the Oedipal triangular model. Indeed, it almost seems like a caricature that the boy's relationship to his frail mother is defined by a very close attachment, while his respect for his father is laden with fear.[31] And on this basis, the land surveyor is soon misled to assume that it is not Hans's intention to offer help: the boy is there for the very opposite reason, unwittingly looking for help against his father.[32] With this assumption the interrogation situation alters into an anamnesis. Abruptly, K. mentions his medical knowledge and experience in treating sicknesses, and later the boy observes the land surveyor as if he were "a doctor who is lost in thought in an effort to find a cure for a serious case."[33] Eventually, in the therapeutic setting, which gradually entices Hans to become more talkative, a classical transference takes place. Without thinking all that much, i. e. on the path of free association, the boy says he would like to become a man like K. For his part, the land surveyor, perceiving himself to be trapped in a contemptible and by no means enviable situation, ponders this wish and in a somewhat painstaking interpretative reflection comes to the conclusion that Hans must have placed him, K., in the imaginary position of an omnipotent father. The chapter, which to the very end refrains from betraying any definitive knowledge about the child, ends with this hypothesis.

Against the background of these borrowings of motifs from Freudian psychoanalysis,[34] the following key considerations emerge, underpinning that through the link to little Hans, the episode from *The Castle* is understandable as a case history. Firstly, Kafka takes up the merging of *casus* and *lapsus* by characterizing the boy as a "schwerer Fall," a "serious case" or literally as suffering from a "severe fall," a phrase that subtly connects the case history with the gravitational pull of plunging. Parallel to Freud, Kafka also dissects the dream of

the paradisiac angel, as a significant remark from the Oedipus story *The Judgment* shows, wherein Georg Bendemann is
judged by his father, who claims: "An innocent child, yes, that
you were, truly, but still more truly have you been a devilish
human being."[35] Secondly, the Hans chapter is a case history
because Kafka marks the singular case data as a linguistic
lacuna that threatens to epistemically sabotage the *casus*. For
this reason, the case history cannot avoid but "to portray the
more general." Kafka's story also revolves around a genuinely
childhood liminal experience with the transition into the symbolic order—it is thus no coincidence that the boy in the episode from *The Castle* is introduced in detail after entering the
schoolroom. With this interest in scenarios of beginnings, the
Hans chapter is part of a broadly-based casuistry in Kafka's
work, alertly tracing the forming of cultural orders and impli-
cating the scarcely accessible domain of the pre-symbolic.[36]

Despite all these common features, the discursive framework in which Kafka and Freud respectively operate needs to
be distinguished. With his regiment of observers, the psycho-
analyst is taking part in an overarching project that, since the
nineteenth century, has set about empirically exploring the
nature of children on the basis of scientific criteria. Emerging in the process is what nascent developmental psychology
then declares openly, namely the fact that, for the first time in
the history of childhood in the Modern Age, infantility comes
into focus detached from questions of education and family.
Although Kafka's texts result in the same outcome, the writer
starts from a different observation, seeing the child exposed
to an omnipresent crossfire of institutional power relations.
It is no coincidence that the Hans chapter frames the therapeutic scene with a school interrogation situation, and shows
how a child in need is at the mercy of adult interests, or to use

Frieda's dramatic words, is "abused." The strength to refuse to comply to the norms of the institution is entrusted fully to the infantile.

Moreover, a systematic aspect results from the difference of the discursive rules, one that impacts on the dynamic of the narration. While Freud mentions the shortage of information as an operative problem in analyzing a child, but then casts it aside in favor of the theoretic interest,[37] Kafka's writing resolutely holds on to the secret of childhood. A lacuna delimited in this way continues to unfurl an effect, so that the irretrievable origin entails a potentially endless series of stories. In Freud, this concatenation is only visible because the case of little Hans basically contains not one but two stories, namely those of the first and the second observer. In contrast, Kafka's episode from *The Castle* is just one in an open-ended series of several Hans stories.

## III.

One of Hans's first appearances in Kafka's work is an entry in the Octavo Notebook A from 1916–1917. Entitled "In the Attic," the sketched scenario presages an allegory of childhood:

> The children had a secret. In the attic, in a far corner, among all the rubbish accumulated during a whole century, where no adult could grope his way in any more, Hans, the advocate's son, had discovered a strange man. He was sitting on a chest, which was propped up against the wall, lying on its side. When he caught sight of Hans, his face showed neither fright nor astonishment, only apathy; he met Hans's gaze with clear eyes. A big round cap

made of Crimean lambskin was pulled far down on his head. He had a thick mustache, which stood out stiffly. He was wearing a loose brown cloak held together by a tremendous system of straps, reminiscent of a horse's harness [...] "Go away!" Hans screamed, as the man stretched out his hand slowly to take hold of him; he ran far away into the newer parts of the attic and stopped only when the wet washing, hung up there to dry, slapped into his face. But then, after all, he turned straight back again. [...] So Hans risked pushing aside an old fire screen, riddled with holes, that was still separating him from the stranger, and went quite close up to him and finally indeed touched him. [...] "I'm Hans," he said, "the advocate's son. And who are you?" "I see," the stranger said, "I am Hans too, my name's Hans Schlag, I'm a huntsman from Baden and come from Kossgarten on the Neckar. Old stories."[38]

This allegory contours childhood as an unfathomable secret. In terms of imagery this is expressed through the attic figuring as a heterotopy, one adults no longer have access to. The prevailing laws of space and time seem suspended in this children's realm. The advocate's son Hans discovers here amongst the clutter of used and meanwhile useless things a huntsman from a past era. This strange man is wearing a loose brown cloak, and the straps holding it together remind the boy of a horse harness. The allusion to Freud's case history is apparent and explains why at first the child runs away frightened. Gradually though, Hans musters his courage and dares to speak to the stranger. As the conclusion of the sketch makes clear, here a little Hans is encountering an older Hans. This not only underlines that Hans is a name for every one and no one. What is even more pivotal is that Kafka moves forward from one Hans story to the next.[39] As the Octavo Notebooks B and D show, the present scene is the first sketch of the *Hunter Gracchus* story. The old stories the strange man mentions and which refer to a mythical origin are, significantly, about a fall: the hunter Gracchus has fallen from a rocky outcrop and died. Since then he has been journeying on his "death boat," having missed the turn into the Orcus, and continues to travel on through the world, neither fully dead or alive, without ever reaching redemption. With this narrative sequence Kafka translates Freud's children's story into a multiplicity of interrelated Hans stories which reflect the *casus* as a lapse.[40]

In this chapter, I have sought to shed light on the genre of the case history, which as Foucault identified, had started to proliferate rapidly in the eighteenth century on the back of a genuinely modern interest in human individuality, by considering the—for the discourse historian exemplary—case of little Hans. The starting point for the comparison between the Hans stories of Freud and Kafka was the observation that the psychoanalytical *casus* had left traces behind in the writer's work—traces which indicate a scarcely perceptible but subtle reception of Freudian psychoanalysis. Both authors share the new interest in children that shapes several discourses around 1900. Not only psychoanalysis and literature, but at the threshold to the new century developmental and experimental psychology and progressive education also embark on the project to enter the practically inaccessible realm of childhood. An understanding is perceivable in both Kafka and Freud that breaks with the Romantic idealization and presents the child as a fallen angel. But the differences are not to be neglected. Freud takes the case of little Hans to be an example of child sexuality and the neurotic entanglements of Oedipus. Although his case history takes into consideration the difficulties in ascertaining the true essence of the individual, with an authorial gesture he pushes this problem into the background. This approach may be seen as stemming logically from the discursive rules for furnishing a scientific case history. As Foucault and in his wake cultural studies in recent years have pointed out, while the *casus* tells the story of an abnormal individual, the empirical data is always also, and indeed above all, interested in finding generalizable insights and regularities.[41] In contrast, the case history told in literature is free of such a prescriptive orientation, simply because the purposes and aims of literature are "less practical than those of other discourses."[42] Kafka can thus insist that little Hans and childhood in general remain incomprehensible, meaning that he can also leave behind the guiding distinction of "health/illness" that is decisive for medical cases. In the light of Kafka's reception, the more or less blind spots of the scientific *casus* become transparent; and moreover, Kafka's stories of little Hans underline a factor considered neither by Foucault nor scholarly discourse—the case of fallen humans can be told ever anew and again, differently each time.

Fɪɢ. 8: Henri Cartier-Bresson, *Moment in Time* (1971).

# This Briefest Childhood (*Kafka*)

## I.

Greek Antiquity provides us with a figure that is extraordinary and singular in the history of conceptions of time. A fragment from Heraclitus, B 52, reads: "Aion is a child at play, gambling; a child's is the kingship" (αἰὼν παῖς ἐστι παίζων, πεσσεύων· παιδὸς ἡ βασιληίη). The saying—how could it be any different with Heraclitus—is extremely concise and enigmatic.[1] The mysteriousness stems from how the meaning of the word "aion" evades precise definition in its pre-Socratic usage. It is only with Plato's distinction between "aion" and "chronos," i.e. between ideational and immovable time and physical and movable time, introduced in *Timaeus*, that the concept becomes philosophically codified, launching it on a career which, through a series of misunderstandings in the neo-Platonic, Greco-Judeo, and Christian tradition, has led to the still prevailing notion of "eon," "eternity," and "imperishability."[2] According to this tradition, "aion" merely means an unbounded expanse of time and thus represents only a quantitative difference to "chronos"; "aion" is, to draw on a phrase from the *Septuagint*, "megas aion," an "immense time," and means the transcendent state of a fulfilled existence.[3] This contrasts to the pre-Socratic usage, decisively influenced by Homer. Homer understands the word in the sense of "life" or "life force," and employs it, as the study by Conrad Lackeit from 1916 appreciates, "only in relationship to the end of life, to death."[4] "Aion" thus means a quantitatively smaller time span, namely that of a lifetime limited by death. Accordingly, most interpretations of the Heraclitus fragment unhesitatingly see the child *Aion* as the uncontrollable and "random play of becoming and perishing," the tragic fate of human finitude.[5] The poetic personification—Lackeit's study underlines that prior to Plato "aion" is a word exclusively used poetically—, the imagery of the child and its kingly play, still remains in need of explanation against this background, for the qualitative difference to "chronos," inherent to both Plato's and Heraclitus's concept of "aion," remains unconsidered. Without furnishing an answer in a doctrinal sense, Heraclitus's fragment prompts a question: what does the playing child do with (life-) time?

The following considerations take up this question, examining its relevance for literary reflections on "childhood" in Franz Kafka's works. For this purpose, beginning with the *Gracchus* sketches from the early Octavo Notebooks from 1916–1917 (II.) and proceeding on to the clearly discernible influence of Nietzsche's reading of Heraclitus (III.), before culminating in the "briefest childhood" in Kafka's last story, *Josephine the Singer, or the Mouse Folk* from 1924 (IV.), I propose to elaborate an aionic temporality as the characteristic feature of Kafka's conception of childhood (V.), a temporality that is not a static and transcendent eternity but a playful, poetic disruptive work on *chronos* and, moreover, is revealing in view of Kafka's peculiar reflections on time in the later Octavo Notebooks from 1917–1918 (VI.).

## II.

The second detailed sketch from Octavo Notebook B of 1916–1917 opens with a sentence that is to be read in direct connection with Heraclitus's fragment B 52 and with which the texts gathered under the title *The Hunter Gracchus* in the established editions commence: "Two boys were sitting on the harbor wall playing with dice."[6] The scene depicts a deathly still small harbor and is set in a place called "Riva." Appearing to refer to the well-known village on Lake Garda,[7] this name is simply the Italian word for "shore," and it is here, on this shore, that two boys are playing while sitting on a "harbor"—or to take up the original German ("Quaimauer")— "quay wall," whereby *le quai* is the French word for "dock" or "shore." The inlet into the text, which—given that the *Gracchus* sketches demonstrate neither a definitive beginning nor an end[8]—one can perhaps more succinctly call a "text shore," has astonishingly failed to attract any attention in the voluminous secondary literature on this enigmatic text.[9] Against the background of our considerations, the reference to the ancient figuration of *Aion* is hardly surprising. Analyzing the ensuing sentence from a perspective aware of the aforementioned temporal relationships, it is then patently clear, beyond the link between motifs, that the philosophical figure of a playing child is evoked. In the critical edition, the text opens with the sentences: "Two boys were sitting on the harbor wall playing with dice. A man was reading a newspaper on the steps of the monument, resting in the shadow of a hero who was flourishing his sword on high."[10] This passage contains two contrary manifestations of "time:" firstly, in the form of the monument to a hero, whereby the practical and documentary quality produces what is generally called "history," namely the history of glorious and grand deeds, the so-called *res gestae*; and secondly, the "newspaper," which literally follows in the footsteps of history, in Kafka's image aptly positioned on the steps of the monument, the newspaper indicating datable time as a measurable rhythm of days and weeks.

This second sentence reveals several differences to the first. One is marked by how there is the small world of the children and the large world of the adults: while the boys are sitting on the quay wall, i.e. the shore, and playing dice, an adult is positioned in the direct vicinity of a monument. Another is how both sentences are bound to varying time spheres. While dice is characteristic of an activity, subject to the whims of the children, without defined beginning and without a motivated end, the second sentence denotes a chronologically countable time, which stands for a continuum of before and after. Although the difference still needs to be elaborated in detail, here we may already assume two times which need to be distinguished qualitatively, namely a brief time of children and a long time of adults.

Kafka's revision of the second sentence sheds light on how these two spheres are in conflict. Initially it read: "A man sat on the steps of a monument in the shadow of a hero swinging a sabre and read a newspaper."[11] Through the the conjuction of two cola, this base text renders discernible a course of events marked by a narrative sequence of before and after. The revision with its reduction to a single colon transforms the sentence into a tableau and appears to convey an immobilized present. This phenomenon is to be found with other changes through the *Gracchus* sketch, testifying to Kafka's effort to also create an impression of the timeless and immobile on the stylistic level—the cinematographic slow motion of the opening visualizes petrified time: "A bark quietly floated into the small harbor as if borne above the water."[12]

Reading the base text of the inlet while taking into account the deletion, a tension in the narrative configuring of time emerges, namely the coexistence of two contrary time spheres, or the opposition between purposeful movement, i.e. "action," on the one hand, and slowed movement on the other. On the thematic level, these contrastive time forms fundamentally determine the death passage of the undead Gracchus, endlessly swaying between the antithesis of calm and movement: having taken a wrong turn while on its way to the next world, the huntsman's ship journeys on and on with "no rudder,"[13] "sometimes up, sometimes down, sometimes on the right, sometimes on the left, always in motion,"[14] until its arrival in Riva, with the huntsman lying there "without motion and, it seemed, without breathing, his eyes closed [...]."[15]

In its description of children playing and the monument to the hero and the newspaper, the inlet into the text thus figuratively ignites the tension between purposefully directed and directionless movement. It is as if Kafka had playfully rolled two temporal conceptions like dice[16] in the first two sentences and evoked the elementary dual problematic for the following pages: firstly, that time is structurally bifurcated;[17] and secondly, that chronological time is disrupted and modified in its linear and continuous course by the play of *Aion*.

Ridden with tension, this relationship remains virulent for the composition of this *Gracchus* sketch from the Octavo Notebook B through to the very end, and hence directly impacts on Kafka's writing: i.e. the organization, which has now become problematic, into a "story." It is thus by no means a coincidence that the sketch abruptly ends with words usually employed to set a plot in motion: "I lay down and waited. Then it happened."[18] What is interrupted in the middle of the sentence is the opening to a plot sequence and chronological order which could have fitted together into a story, one however that remains blocked.

Against the background of the time problematic prominent in the first two sentences, the critical *constitutio* of a

consistent text completely misses the point, for it simply elim-
inates the decisive tension the sketch initiates without finding a solution and an end. The *Huntsman Gracchus* complex
brings together a series of sketches and drafts unpublished
by Kafka in his lifetime, their motifs more or less interrelated,
but obviously lacking coherency, i.e. the linearity and enclosed
unity necessary for a "story,"[19] and in which rather moments
of the discontinuous, the interrupted, and the inconsistent
are intrinsic.[20] This is not to be put down to the writer's lack of
skill; instead, considering the poetological reflection evident
in the manuscripts, its source is to be found and analyzed in
the aionic time of childhood.

The tension between these different times is already pre-
saged in the first *Gracchus* draft from the Octavo Notebook A,
and here too a child plays the main role. It is no coincidence
that it is the young boy Hans who encounters a huntsman
from another age in the attic. The stranger is found sitting
at a place where adults expressly can no longer "grope" their
way to, namely "[a]mong the junk of an entire century stored
in the the attic, in a deep nook [...]."[21] In the attic, where only
used and meanwhile useless objects and protagonists from
past epochs are to be found, a different order of time reigns,
one that cannot be dated chronologically, and hence, in other
words, represents a dis-ordering of time. This realm of childhood envelops within it the secret of a specific time, a time that
is taken up again in the *Gracchus* draft from Octavo Notebook
B and remains present in other sketches from the notebooks,
evidently wherever children and their games are named and
staged. Before looking at these scenes in more detail, it seems
advisable to gain a more specific idea of what constitutes this
childhood realm, for which a small excursus is necessary.

## III.

A prominent rewriting of Heraclitus's fragment B 52 is to be found in Friedrich Nietzsche's *Philosophy in the Tragic Age of the Greeks* from 1873, a work left incomplete and unpublished in his lifetime. Integral to his intensive study of the pre-Socratics,[22] "Nietzsche's interpretation of Heraclitus thus focuses on"[23] a longer passage on *Aion*:

> A Becoming and Passing, a building and destroying, without any moral bias, in perpetual innocence is in this world only the play of the artist and of the child. And, similarly, just as the child and the artist play, the eternally living fire plays, builds up and destroys, in innocence—and this game the Æon plays with himself. Transforming himself into water and earth, like a child he piles heaps of sand by the sea, piles up and demolishes; from time to time he recommences the game. A moment of satiety, then again desire seizes him, as desire compels the artist to create.[24]

Taking up a reference from Jacob Bernays,[25] Nietzsche is reworking here a passage from the *Iliad*—and in view of Kafka's boys sitting on the quay wall, this veiled reference is striking, for in the Homeric scene Apollo, the god of the arts, is compared to a child playing on the seashore.[26] Nietzsche's aesthetic interpretation of the Heraclitus saying describes a creation and destruction in the child's action that is innocent because it occurs outside the boundaries defined by the means-purpose schema postulated in moral philosophy.[27] Without any identifiable goal, this act of play, following the law of chance, is repeated all over again—the same phenomenon is also expressed in a later notebook entry, existence framed in terms of a "great game of chance" and the world as repeating itself infinitely in a never-ending "circular movement."[28] With this equation between child and artist, Nietzsche is taking up a topos that emerged with the discovery of childhood in the eighteenth century, but became particularly powerful in Romanticism and traditionally idealized the natural, spontaneous, and innocent creativity of a child's imagination into the origin of the poetic.[29] For Nietzsche too, the child and the artist are both moved by a ludic drive—but "other worlds" are only created to the extent that these new universes are then in turn destroyed. And it is not a child-artist who is in charge when playing, but rather an uncontrollable becoming and passing are at work. The game draws in the players, engrossing them fully, and there is thus no space available for aesthetic freedom. In this sense, play is not some privileged cultural practice that, in the wake of German classicist aesthetics, can be claimed to be a specifically human activity.[30] For Nietzsche, child creativity only takes place as part of a circular movement, as a moment in a cycle in which nothing—neither the subject nor the product of its creating—survives. The work created by a child is defined by an inherent negation of itself. Later, in *Zarathustra*, a work Kafka read early in his life and greatly admired,[31] the play of the child is described as "a wheel rolling out of itself" and a constantly "new beginning,"[32] as a game in which there is no sovereign subject and in which linear time is suspended.[33]

According to Nietzsche, art needs to be thought of as an aionian realm, one in which the play of a child brings forth—in time—a specific structure. This temporal dimension can be described as the repetition, grounded in itself and without purpose and norm, of creation and destruction. And in this repetition, the subject and the work yielded only play a role in terms of ensuring their own negation.

## IV.

Kafka addressed the topos of the infantile artist in his last story, *Josephine the Singer, or the Mouse Folk* (1924), which in many respects corresponds to Nietzsche's aesthetic determination of child play, while however decidedly placing the aspect of time in the foreground. What links the singer Josephine with the Heraclitean tradition is the problem of "childtime"—the time granted to be a child—which the narrative expressly addresses in terms of the protagonist's artistic activity. Josephine's singing, as Walter Benjamin was the first to point out, has "something of our poor brief childhood, something of lost happiness which can never be found again."[34] An infantility is at work in her feeble and scarcely perceptible singing that is, to start with, so precarious because it is granted no place as a genuinely experienced time in the life of mice. The pertinent passage reads:

> Among our people there is no age of youth, scarcely the briefest childhood. Regularly, it is true, demands are put forward that the children should be granted a special freedom, a special protection, that their right to be a little carefree, to have a little senseless giddiness, a little play, that this right should be respected and the exercise of it encouraged [...]. Our life happens to be such that a child, as soon as it can run about a little and a little distinguish one thing from another, must look after itself just like an adult; the areas on which, for economic reasons, we have to live in dispersion are too wide, our enemies too numerous, the dangers lying everywhere in wait for us too incalculable—we cannot shelter our children from the struggle for existence, if we did so, it would bring them to an early grave. These depressing considerations are reinforced by another, which is not depressing: the

fertility of our race. One generation—and each is numerous—treads on the heels of another, the children have no time to be children. Other races may foster their children carefully, schools may be erected for their little ones, out of these schools the children may come pouring daily, the future of the race, yet among them it is always the same children that come out day after day for a long time. We have no schools, but from our race come pouring out at the briefest of intervals the innumerable swarms of our children, merrily lisping or chirping so long as they cannot yet pipe [...]. And not the same children, as in those schools, no, always new children again and again, without end, without a break, hardly does a child appear than it is no more a child, while behind it new childish faces are already crowding so fast and so thick that they are indistinguishable, rosy with happiness. Truly, however delightful this may be and however much others may envy us for it, and rightly, we simply cannot give a real childhood to our children.[35]

Unlike those societies in which childhood is assigned a specific time and exact place, the mice children move immediately into adulthood without any transitional phase. As in premodern cultures, this mouse state seems to offer no space of protection where its inhabitants could be carefree and without the burdens of worry, for the sheer struggle to survive forces the animals to skip childhood: "Children aren't given the time to be children" is a formulation that, by no means accidentally, renders this situation in temporal terms. So, how are we to understand this "briefest childhood"? Most obviously to the effect that this time simply does not exist, in the sense that it would be chronologically comprehensible through a traditional segmenting of a lifetime into "childhood"—"adulthood"—"old age" and thus represent a real period of time in the life of a mouse. The time lived by the mice has no interruption and no development; a constant and endless becoming reigns, and no individuality is brought forth. The "briefest childhood" Kafka speaks of cannot mean a delimited and substantially determined chronological-biographical stage in the history of a subject, i.e. the childhood that, since the eighteenth century, with the establishment of bourgeois society, with the nuclear family and school, was defined and set into institutional forms as the rudimentary foundations for the individual. Threatened by radical disappearance, childhood in the mice folk is, in a peculiar way, set in relationship to aesthetic considerations on the protagonist's singing.

As a result of a childhood that fails to take place, the mice are paradoxically pervaded by an "ineradicable childishness."[36] This infantility is at odds with the practical common sense in mice and is expressed in foolish, wasteful, and senseless—in short: playful—actions. The impact of this specific mouse child-time thus becomes all the greater the more it withdraws—the briefer it is, the more powerful its presence.[37] It does not lie in the past as a finished stage, but is present precisely because it has never taken place. And so it gradually emerges that this briefest childhood is not a quantitative but a qualitative specification. Childhood plays a role precisely because it cannot be measured on the criteria of chronological time. According to this logic, it marks a gap in the temporal continuum, one in which another time dimension opens up, namely, as with the playing boy *Aion*, that of child's play.

Something of this playing not only remains always present in the ineradicable childishness of the mice—it is also a source nourishing Josephine's art. According to reports, her singing has always profited from the specific childishness of her people,[38] and in such a way that infantility brings forth a negative impact. Josephine's weak piping, which in fact "is no piping," this "frail little voice"[39] of hers, is described as a "mere nothing in voice,"[40] her music accordingly "reduced to the least possible trace."[41] Josephine's artful play is not enacted as childish because—as the Romantic topos would demand—it is especially creative, genial, and original, but rather because of a contrary quality: how it displays an inner intractability of what it is to be a child, and draws on this for sustenance. To come to grips with the status of infantility in Franz Kafka's writings therefore requires a conception of "childhood" that goes decidedly beyond pedagogy and developmental psychology.

## V.

The inconspicuous appearance of children in the Octavo Notebooks is related—from the perspective of the briefest childhood in the *Josephine* story—not gratuitously with the disappearing and yet omnipresent presence of infantile beings in Kafka's writings. Alongside well-known and poetologically pivotal texts like *The Cares of a Family Man*[42] from 1917 and *The Top* from 1920,[43] both of which posit the radical impossibility of gaining knowledge about the infantile, the marginal position accorded children in the Octavo Notebooks needs to be grasped more precisely in several aspects. Of fundamental significance is how "childhood" emerges as a poetological conception, and precisely where a child's relationship to language is the topic, when for example the dialogue partner of the huntsman Gracchus is described as "a babbling child"[44] or when the "[m]urmuring of the children"[45] is mentioned. As already observed with respect to Josephine's singing, namely that it includes the mute space prior to articulation and that her piping constantly hovers on the verge of piping, Kafka also stages the language of the *infantes* in the liminal realm to non-language.

In fact, in the Octavo Notebooks children appear systematically in mute threshold realms. As early as the very first page in Octavo Notebook A—the poetological fragment *Steadfast Dream*—, they are standing motionless "in the doors,"[46] while at the beginning of Octavo Notebook B they are playing on the quay wall, and capturing interest in Octavo Notebook C is a set of steps, their origin proving to be a mystery: in the vague recollection of the first-person narrator they surface in nothing less than a children's book, out of which the steps seem to have directly arisen.[47]

The children in the Octavo Notebooks move not only in spatial thresholds but also in intermediate temporal zones, and it is striking that this is always whenever they appear at the side of the dead. In Octavo Notebook F for example, a child directly describes the following situation: "Once a coffin with a corpse lay at our place for a whole night—I don't remember the reason. For us, the gravedigger's children, there was nothing strange about coffins; when we went to sleep we hardly thought about the fact that there was a corpse in the same room."[48] The scene is only uncanny on the surface—i.e. in the eyes of adults—because corpses obviously pose no threat to children. One reason for this is how, as documented in cultural history, children and the deceased are assigned an equivalent place in a system that juxtaposes the world of the dead and the world of the living.[49] Birth and death mark the critical moment of transition from one world to the other. As the deceased have traveled the path from life to death, the threshold realm from birth into life is marked by childhood. Because birth does not directly produce grownup adults but children, they mark a critical passage, one that relates to the change from the human time of chronologically measurable motion to the unmovable eternal time of the dead and vice versa.

Perhaps this perspective, which while mythical is relevant in cultural history,[50] can shed some light on the disconcerting presence of children in the *Gracchus* fragments, above all the crowd of small boys who accompany the presumably dead huntsman from the harbor to the yellow house, where the funeral is to take place, and form a guard of honor along the way.[51] Numbering about fifty, no one knows where they've come from. They are obviously part of a ritual and attend to the function of ensuring that the deceased pass safely into the world of the dead. The purpose of mourning rites is then fulfilled when the delicate passage into a definitive state is deliberately and attentively completed and the deceased become the dead. Without a ritual, i.e. without a defined relationship to the realm of the dead, the deceased, threatening and homeless specters, roam the world of the living. Precisely because death endangers the stable opposition erected between the worlds of the living and the dead, the ritual must ensure that the passage is completed, thus consolidating the binary system.

And it is precisely this rite that goes awry in *Gracchus*, interrupted the moment the motionless huntsman opens his eyes like a zombie. Because a way has yet to be found to guide the huntsman definitively into the realm of the dead, bringing to a standstill his perpetual journey, the binary system is suspended. Gracchus finds himself in an intermediate realm— still on this side while on the way to the afterlife.

**150**

This passage from the world of the living into that of dead is marked by a specific temporality. Ever since his death, the story has ceased to proceed in "good order"[52] for the huntsman. The chronological-linear course of events, having defined the story of his life and now suddenly no longer ensured, seems to have simply come to an end. But because he is yet to arrive in the realm of the dead, for Gracchus time continues to lapse and is yet to fully come to a standstill. And so on he moves in a "time between," which may be described as a kind of paralysis of chronological time. At the beginning of the *Gracchus* fragment from Octavo Notebook B, this "time between" features as the game of dice played by the boys and, moreover, is evoked in a slow-motion depiction. The elongating of time taking place in child play produces an intensified presentness, with the past and the future forgotten. "Riva," with its scores of children, suddenly appearing from seemingly nowhere, two of whom play dice, while around fifty accompany a "dead" man, is Kafka's poetic figuration of the kingdom of *Aion*.

## VI.

The interpretation of the *Huntsman Gracchus* sketches in terms of temporality can be contextualized through Kafka's broadly-based work on the concept of "time" in the Octavo Notebooks. At the center of the undertaking is the effort to overcome the prevailing, i.e. the chronological, notion of time. Located in Octavo Notebook G is the famous philosophical note on history: "The decisive moment in human evolution is perpetual."[53] As the boy *Aion* rolls the dice, letting it "fall," for Kafka the progression of time in child's play is "perpetual," i.e. not once and for all, but again and again, paralyzed.[54] For the purpose of a conception of history that supersedes metaphysical ideas of "progress," "development," and "final goal," of "beginning" and "end" with the "perpetual instant" and the "still-standing storm," Kafka resorts however to Messianic props, which he then translates into a specific aesthetic of child's play in his concerted reception of the Heraclitean tradition and aionic time. This is also of central importance for Kafka's literary practice, where the salient concepts of time like "story" and "action," "beginning" and "end" become textual problems. Where most of the writings left unpublished by Kafka transgress the accepted norms of textuality in terms of their beginning- and endlessness, their narrative inconsistency and textual brittleness, then this stems from a literary practice that takes the time to play like children.

Likewise, in the context of modern literature, the traditional concept of "childhood" needs to be overhauled. While dominant childhood discourses like pedagogy, psychology, and sociology focus on the child in such a way that it must completely leave behind its childhood from a specific point of time onwards in order to become a grownup human being, Kafka's infantile protagonists remain untouched by such a prescribed development. At the same time, his children are not idealized in line with the topos of Romanticism into paradisiacal poets, nor emphatically posited as the lost origin of humanness and culture. Defying or eluding domination and control by the institutions of the family and school, Kafka's children engage instead in a game that is played out at the boundaries of the subject, of time, and of art, its effect both destructive and productive. Standing outside the definitions of moral philosophy, this game is located this side of the classical distinction to earnestness. Neither earnest play nor playful earnestness, it signifies an activity, increasingly threatened by disappearance, for which no concept stands readily available for adults.

# An Angel's Grace, a Devil's Grin

## I.

What is a child? For us moderns, the answer seems self-evident. We all think we know what a child is. We can all match, with a good deal of certainty, human individuals to this social category. A child represents what we once were, but no longer are. Childhood is a designation usually covering the phase from birth to the onset of puberty, through which we, progressing in terms of our ontogenetic development, enter the stage of adolescence. In terms of the ages of life, in turn adolescence is conceived of as the transition into adulthood, which comes to an end in the final phase of life as we arrive at old age. According to this classical model, the child stands for the beginnings of human development, so that by definition we, as children, are not—or not yet—what we one day will be.

Considered in the light of the literary discourse, the question as to what a child is certainly confronts us with difficulties. At least this is how the German writer Marie Luise Kaschnitz felt, who explored in diverse ways the motifs associated with the child and childhood in her work, in particular during the postwar years.[1] A diary entry from the late 1960s recalls an attempt to write a poem entitled *Was ist ein Kind* (*What is a Child*):

> Sometimes I note down titles for poems I intend to write, sooner or later. Today I found, on a slip of paper, the title: *What is a child*, and beneath it the words, Midesa baby food, baby seats for the car, every child a Christ child, every child a murderer, don't

cross the street when it's red, psalms-palms. I've got no idea how
I wanted to make sense out of all that.[2]

These lines are much like the minutes noting a sudden poetic idea never sculpted into the form of a finished poem. A
varied mix of fleeting associations are captured which lead,
directly and surprisingly, from the food industry and the
market tailored to meeting the specific needs of bringing up
a child through to religious and anthropological assertions,
and these in turn stand seemingly without any semblance of
a connection next to a domain of order, law, and discipline.
Finally, what one normally expects from a poem is expressed,
namely a rhyme, "psalms/palms," quite obviously taking up a
linking of Christian ideas, but in fact inducing the author to
the counterfactual observation that she no longer knows how
all this was to be brought together to make sense, or literally
in the German "zusammenreimen," "to be rhymed together."
*What is a child*—it appears not as simple as it seems to weave
a meaningful rhyme in response to this question.

The failure of a poem to emerge from these minutes is
not due to the writer's lack of poetical ability; it stems rather
from an erroneous framing of the question—at its very fundamental level, the question needs to be posed differently. As it
is formulated, it immediately suggests that the answer lies in
some essentialism, and in the case of childhood this is plainly
unfeasible. In truth, the associations listed in the diary entry
in fact challenge the assumption that one could say what in
essence a child is. Things and ideas are mentioned which
prompt us to conclude that the child is to be defined through
economic, religious, anthropological, and social norms, of
which it is only logical to assume that they are historically and
culturally variable. The terms listed in the diary entry indicate

that childhood needs to be approached and considered as an idea for which religious models are of importance. But not only that—these ideas are also highly ambivalent: "Every child a Christ child, every child a murderer" stand side by side in the greatest contrast imaginable.

How is it possible that Kaschnitz reflects on the child as a Christ child and murderer at once? The considerations elaborated in this chapter start from the assumption that far more needs to be described and explained here than just some poetic idiosyncrasy. We are dealing, firstly, with an ambiguity that increasingly pushes to the fore as the literature of Modernism unfolds; and secondly, because a cultural matrix is discernible in the ambivalence that is of fundamental significance for the occidental discourse on childhood, a matrix that is by no means limited to the images and conceptions of childhood evident in Antiquity, the Middle Ages, or even especially theology. On the contrary: It is clear that religious ideas and concepts in relation to the child continued to have a lasting effect in the secular Modern epoch, when they indeed experienced a new boom. To the extent that the child in the bourgeois age becomes the focus of attention as a being of infinite determinability, then it is accordingly exposed to starkly contrastive, if not contradictory interpretations, which, oscillating between divinization and demonization, have maintained a formative influence on the cultural imagination of the Western world down to the present day.

## II.

As described by Philippe Ariès, the "discovery of childhood" is characterized by the persistence of religious ideas and motifs whose occidental roots lie in the Christian heritage. The centering of social concern around the child goes hand in hand with its symbolic sacralization, and this sacralization can draw on the New Testament and its stock tradition of images and ideas. Ariès discerns this connection in the chapter entitled "from immodesty to innocence," tracing the crystallization and propagation of the idea of the child's sexual innocence, which had, so he claims, been very alien to premodern cultures.[3] In this context, for the Early Modern period he notes a close relationship between the "devotion to the Holy Childhood and the great development of interest in childhood, of the provision of the little schools and colleges, and of educational theory," which would emerge soon after.[4] According to Ariès, the growing interest in the young since the seventeenth century leads to granting the child a new and pivotal place; significantly, this not only occurs in religious life and iconography but also in secular contexts, the revaluation of childhood further ennobled by "Christ's childhood," and in a way that the moderns, unlike all before them, believe to glimpse in infants and children the angelic "reflection of divine purity."[5] Christian ideas and sentiments not only obviously persist in the secular Modern Age, but are indeed recoded and intensified.

Ariès's findings are more appreciable and understandable when they are considered in the broader framework of a significant sacralization of the bourgeois nuclear family. As Albrecht Koschorke has shown, the New Testament family story revolving around the infant Jesus by no means became obsolete in secular times; rather, in the form of an epilogue it remained so virulent that the model of the Holy Family has continued to inspire the collective imagination, leaving an indelible mark on the discourse of Enlightenment, the nineteenth century with its steadfast belief in the efficacy of science, and through to contemporary Hollywood cinema. This transfer between the divine and profane spheres possesses a constitutive significance for the genealogy of the bourgeois nuclear family, already evident in programmatic writings from the Early Modern period. Discernible in Luther for instance is a manifest "redirecting of sacred energies into secular institutions," which will then become formative for the establishment of the family order in later times.[6] Concretely, this means that, on the path to the secular Modern Age, married life is modelled on the stereotype of the Holy Family and rigorously committed to achieving a pious nearness to God:

> Protestant writings proclaimed the active and productive domestic life as a whole to be a service to God. Families were nothing less than "little churches." According to social historian Lawrence Stone, domestic piety "filled the vacuum left by the decline of the Church and its priests," along with the public ritual acts they performed. Referring to developments in England, Stone speaks of a "general tendency to substitute the household for the church." He concludes: "Thus the Word of God was to some degree removed from the parish church and transferred to the private home: the Holy Spirit was partly domesticated."[7]

If it is correct that one can identify the origins of the modern nuclear family in the first secularization movement of Protestantism, then what emerges here are the beginnings of a process that commences in the Early Modern period, is discursively circulated in the eighteenth century, and then, now firmly anchored in everyday real life, dominates the bourgeois age around and after 1800. From the very outset, the formation of the new family union is thus subject to a "dialectic [...]

between secularization and resacralization,"[8] and this asserts and establishes itself beyond the narrower theological framework of Luther. Like two sides of the same coin, secularization and sacralization are interconnected in the superseding of the old kinship or clan ties. The bourgeois nuclear family is set up as a "little church," and this means: as it is founded as a secular holy sanctuary, the elements supporting it undergo a recoding that focuses on the core constituents of the new union: father, mother, and child.

According to Koschorke, what is initiated here is a modern transformation of the Holy Family into a secular community, with its members given nothing less than "religious solemnity."[9] This is evident in a number of works of art and literature, the family of the New Testament presented as the model case of the bourgeois family *par excellence* and natural parenthood overlaid with motifs taken from the Mary-Joseph constellation. This involves both the ambiguous divinization of the father in a position that splits between creator and Joseph, as well as the mystification of the mother based on the model of the virgin Madonna and the glorification of the child as the secular savior. This observation is graphically demonstrated in Rembrandt's depictions of the life of the Holy Family, which with their everyday realism strikingly present a "naturalization of the holy" and in a host of pictures allow the distinction between the Biblical and bourgeois nuclear family to visually collapse.[10]

As one can see and understand when we keep in mind the propositions put forward by Ariès, Rembrandt's *Holy Family* is characterized by a heightened emotionality towards the child unknown in premodern cultures. As the bourgeois family begins to organize itself around the offspring, so too the affective center of the picture is dominated by the motherly

Fig. 9: Rembrandt, *Holy Family* (1645).

devotion to the newborn, who for its part takes on the role of the infant Jesus in the manger and is enveloped in a sacral aura. All those qualities thus inhere to the small creature which can be inferred from the Christ child: "it is sweet, angelic, heavenly, innocent, sent among humans by God as a supernatural being."[11] For the ideology of childhood propagated by the bourgeois age, this glorification of the familial positions, the successor to Jesus enthroned in the middle, is of eminent significance. To emphasize the point, one could even go so far as to say: the child is the holy of holies to modern culture—not only is the child to bring about an almost heavenly domestic happiness for the family, but also possesses the potential, taking it beyond the familial confines, to play the role of the savior for the whole of humanity.

### III.

As a leading cultural medium of the eighteenth and nineteenth centuries, the literary discourse is instrumental in establishing, consolidating, and problematizing these ideas. Wherever in the wake of Rousseau this discourse discovers the child to be one of its most urgent and crucial themes, the assumption proliferates that, in comparison to civilized adults, the child is quite possibly the better human being and represents a higher form of existence, one that has to serve as the orientation if the depraved present is to be counteracted and a happier future envisioned. An entire literary epoch labors away at this project—commencing with Rousseau in the second half of the eighteenth century, when authors like Herder, Moritz, or Goethe, enter into dialogue with the pedagogic and anthropological writings of the time, turn their attention to the child and recognize its inherent logic. There is no doubt however that the sacralization of the child reaches its highpoint in the literature of Romanticism, wherein a monument of inexhaustible influence is erected to the image of the innocent angelic nature, evident in the works of Novalis, Jean Paul, Brentano, Arnim, Tieck, E.T.A. Hoffmann, and scores of other authors of European Romanticism. Time and again, mythical child figures appear in these texts, presented as miraculous saviors and upon whom nothing less than the hope of redemption from a degenerate reality is pinned. As a host of studies have shown, the period around 1800 is obsessed with the idea of the divine child. What is at play here is a kind of secular eschatology forged on the Christian prototype, and the child now has to not only fulfill the normative demands to be a dutiful and well-behaved innocent being, but also assume the role of secular savior.

This thought-figure can be better understood when we take into consideration the gloomy background it shines from but never fully blends out. As the symptom of a crisis, the belief in the sacral nature of the child is rife, namely in the context of a pathography of the Modern Age, vividly evident for instance in Friedrich Schiller's poetological treatise *On Naïve and Sentimental Poetry* from 1795, a work that provides the Romantics with one of the programmatic impulses for their idea of childhood. Pervaded by the spirit of cultural criticism, Schiller's influential work opens with a caustic diagnosis of the present, identifying a serious malaise. From the outset, children are considered to be the epitome of the naïve, brought into position as the curative antidote to the evils of modern culture, namely the various experiences of alienation from nature, of heteronomy, and of inner divisiveness.[12] "We love in them [i.e. children] the tacitly creative life, the serene spontaneity of their activity, existence in accordance with their own laws, the inner necessity, the eternal unity with themselves."[13] This is how the treatise starts out, with the Heraclitean image of the playing child-king *Aion* also evoked.[14] The starting point is thus marked by noting that beholding simple natural phenomena like plants, animals, or landscapes, and human nature in children or rural people, can produce in us a feeling which gravitates towards the idea of a harmonious unity of humanity at the beginning of time. Unlike Rousseau, Schiller quite clearly emphasizes however that this vision is not directed towards a lost state that can be recovered, but is the construct of a widespread affective disposition, which he, employing the concept of the "sentimental," reflects on as the illness of civilization in the Modern Age, a malady proving extremely difficult to cure. In other words, the naïve is not some regressive fantasy, but a kind of antithetical projection serving therapeutic ends: in contradistinction to the sentimental, the naïve is completely with itself and creates and acts, calmly, out of itself, without even the slightest indication of the dissonance resulting from the break between reason and nature—the naïve is thus balsam for the pathologies of the present age. The positive connotation—promising wholeness—attached to this curative healing accounts for how, as the text continues, the child is glorified into a holy being:

> One is in error to suppose that it is only the notion of helplessness which overcomes us with tenderness at certain moments when we are together with children. That may perhaps be the case with those who in the presence of weakness are accustomed only to feeling their own superiority. But the feeling of which I speak (it occurs only in specifically moral moods and is not to be confused with the emotion that is excited in us by the happy acti-

vity of children) is humiliating rather than favorable to self-love; and even if an advantage were to be drawn from it, this would certainly not be on our side. We are touched not because we look down upon the child from the height of our strength and perfection, but rather because we *look upward* from the *limitation* of our condition, which is inseparable from the *determination* which we have attained, to the unlimited *determinacy* of the child and to its pure innocence; and our emotion at such a moment is too transparently mixed with a certain melancholy for its source to be mistaken. In the child *disposition* and *determination* are represented; in us that *fulfilment* that forever remains far short of those. The child is therefore a lively representation to us of the ideal, not indeed as it is fulfilled, but as it is enjoined; hence we are in no sense moved by the notion of its poverty and limitation, but rather by the opposite: the notion of its pure and free strength, its integrity, its eternality. To a moral and sensitive person a child will be a *sacred* object (ein *heiliger* Gegenstand) [...].[15]

In contrast to the orthodox tradition of the Enlightenment, Schiller's child embodies a higher and not an inferior form of existence, one that represents the idea of a free creative force, of pure innocence, and integrity. Opposing the narrowness of the modern subject, a being of unlimited determinacy is celebrated, and thereby an open playful space of possibility, a space that recalls original human totipotency and predisposes the option of a different, better future. With these coordinates in place, Schiller formulates a mission that shall point the way out of the plight:

They *are* what we *were*; they are what we *once again become*. We were nature just as they, and our culture, by means of reason and freedom, should lead us back to nature. They are, therefore, not

> only the representation of our lost childhood, which eternally remains most dear to us; but fill us with a certain melancholy. But they are also representations of our highest fulfilment in the ideal, hence, thus evoking in us a sublime tenderness.[16]

In this formulation of his philosophy of history, pointedly expressed here and which the Romantics will pursue, Schiller resorts to set pieces from the Christian liturgy, transposing and adapting the phrase usually reserved for Ash Wednesday, *Nam quod es, hoc fueram, quod sum nunc, et eris*.[17] Unlike the religious tradition, which warns of inevitable human decrepitude and ultimately mortality, Schiller is postulating an ideal that transforms Christian Messianism into the secular idea of human perfectibility. To attain highest perfection, the subject of contemporary society must orientate itself on the child it once was in the past and is to once again be in the future. In distinction from Rousseau, Schiller does not lay out a path that ultimately leads back to a primary unity—i.e. takes a circular route—but one that follows a linear teleology. What seems like a return to nature is shown to be a genuinely cultural act, one that has to somehow arrive at childhood harmony and naïvety while staying "on the path of reason and freedom"—i.e. attain a pre-reflective state using the means of reflection, a state only children can represent because "[o]ur childhood is the only undisfigured nature that we still encounter in civilized mankind."[18] This is nothing less than a paradoxical task, eschewing the restitution of a "lost childhood" which is irrecoverably past. "They *are* what we *were*; they are what we *ought to become* once more": adulthood is conceived rather as an indispensable interlude that does not lead back to the original but moves forward into another type of childhood. Novalis will later speak of attaining a "second, higher childhood."[19] In other words: there can be no perfection without undergoing the disconcerting and irreversible experiences of modern culture, which are poison and cure at once. When Schiller imagines a humanity as the ideal goal of this process, which would have succeeded in healing the wounds of reflection and harmonizing the discord inherent to the human species, then with the figure of the child he is not oriented on real life. As is made perfectly clear, the naïve "is *childlikeness where it is no longer expected*, and precisely on this account cannot be ascribed to actual childhood in the most rigorous sense."[20]

With the exaltation of childhood, Schiller—and the Romantics after him—transform the Christian model into a secular narrative which is no less sustained by Messianic hopes. Proceeding from a bleak diagnosis of the contemporary world, the transfiguring character of this idealization is very present in the texts, particularly when they seek salvation in a faraway future and the divine child is entrusted, much like a little savior, with the task of showing the way. Read as the symptom of a crisis, this assumption is the product of a genuinely modern and fundamentally irredeemable emotional disposition. Nevertheless, the idea of the divinity of the child has proved to possess a considerable socio-utopian potential, for instance in the diverse pedagogic programs of the nineteenth and twentieth centuries, which repeatedly evoked the idea of a holy childhood to make it seem practically plausible that a higher level of humanity is only possible through better upbringing and education.[21] Considering the literary texts, strictly speaking this would mean giving the child the sacred freedom in the educational process it is accorded in the conception of the original limitless determinability, and which enables the cultivation of a substantial emptiness in the human being prior to the determinations demanded by social existence. As Schiller sees it, the child is holy because, drawing on the strength of its indeterminacy, in how all determinations, definitions, and identities are deactivated and sublated, it is a bearer of hope.

## IV.

The dark and shadowy sides in the modern imagery of childhood, already present since the Romantics in literary reflection, are not to be interpreted as a contrast to the religious narrative, for the roots of the ambivalences lie in the Christian tradition itself. While the sacralization of the child in the bourgeois age is to be described as the transfer of the salvation historical program structured around the infant Jesus into the secular belief in progress, an ongoing demonization of the child survives in accompaniment, actualizing a model that is just as firmly anchored culturally. This is the adversary to the Messiah, namely Judas Iscariot, who as a "symmetrical negation" is closely intertwined with the fate of the Christian savior.[22]

Epitomizing the wicked child, the narrative of Judas is canonical above all in medieval literature. In his *Legenda aurea*, Jacobus de Voragine tells the story of a villain that does not augur well from the very outset. Analogous to the life of Jesus, the story of Judas begins with a dream his mother Cyborea is supposed to have had shortly before giving birth: "I dreamed that I was going to bear a son so wicked that he would bring ruin upon our whole people."[23] Diametrically opposed to Child Jesus, Judas Iscariot stands for the idea of the ominous child—the child who in its malevolence represents a threat to the whole of humankind, as the legend narrates further:

Already as a child, Judas becomes the devious murderer of his stepbrother, before he, following the tragic fate of Oedipus, unknowingly kills his father and weds his mother, until the eschatological danger he emanates reaches its pinnacle in the betrayal of the son of God. Judas thus comes to fame as the satanic adversary to Jesus, to whom his relationship is a mirror-image inversion, as Koschorke has shown.[24] In the *Divina Commedia*, Dante plots a geometrically exact map of Christian doctrine wherein Judas is assigned his fixed place at the symmetrically opposite pole of the moral order. In the final canto of the *Inferno*, at the very center of hell, where Dante and Virgil catch sight of Lucifer, they recognize the betrayer of all betrayers, Judas, whose head is trapped inside the mouth of the devil. As Satan is the antagonist to God, Judas is the adversary to Jesus; as the latter embodies the principle of the redeeming child, already as a child Judas prefigures the reason causing all damnation.

The discourse of the evil child has a long tradition in cultural history, inherently tied to the theological question of original sin. The Church ritual of baptism draws its motivation from the assumption that the carnal nature of the newborn needs purifying—children who die before baptism accordingly land in limbo, which Dante in turn locates in the first circle of the Inferno, the *limbus puerorum*. The Christian conception of this originary depravation of the child's nature subsequently remained a decisive factor in occidental theories on education until the Modern Age.[25] Protestant pedagogy—beginning with Luther and continuing through the devotional literature of the Early Modern period and on to eighteenth-century pietism—informs its practices, which are anything but accommodating and sensitive, with a particular motivation: because the obstinate will displayed by a child reveals its thoroughly wicked nature, the task is to tame this nature and make it docile. The image of Satan's child in all its variations from the devil's son and the changeling through to the witch child is widespread in these contexts.[26] The reformist pedagogues of the Enlightenment counter this rhetoric of demonization and, following Rousseau, refuse to bow to the doctrine of original sin. Christian Gotthilf Salzmann for example, one of the most prominent advocates of the philanthropic education movement in the second half of the eighteenth century, directly attacks the controversial notion: "There is a hereditary sin, a disposition to evil and an aversion to the good, which children receive from their parents; but it is as such not inborn—but instilled."[27] The offspring is absolved of all guilt because its malice is now no longer considered a natural predisposition but the product of an awry upbringing. And yet, to believe that the religiously-founded idea of the evil child is finished thanks to this Enlightenment discourse is wide of the mark. It now merely becomes rich in variations and more elaborate.

It is not only in pedagogy that all the imperfections of the pupil, which are incompatible with the normative imagery of the innocent angel, now come all the more glaringly to the fore; to an unprecedented degree, the Enlightenment educational doctrine tracked down every hint of an incarnation of evil. The children under the spotlight are those who are savage, insolent, stubborn, greedy, beguiling, disobedient, or in today's terms: difficult and showing behavioral problems or disorders, and who, approached as sinful disruptive factors hindering the secular plan of salvation, are turned into the demonic objects of an arsenal of educational disciplinary techniques, or as they are now known, of "poisonous pedagogy."[28] Depictions and portrayals of the evil child in the literature, cinema, and popular culture of the twentieth and twenty-first centuries are still very much reliant on connotations of the satanic, the eerie, and the monstrous rooted in Christianity.[29] The persistence of this basic religious pattern is traceable in those texts of the Modern Age which, in terms of their own self-understanding, are committed to undertaking a sober and objective analysis—namely, scientific writings on the child. Despite the claims to objectivity, these writings are pervaded and guided by moralistic value judgements and norms of Christian-bourgeois persuasion, which at least in the early stages were unquestioningly accepted.[30]

In stark contrast to the Romantic sacralization of the innocent angel, the sciences at the end of the nineteenth century focus increasingly on the destructive sides of the child's drives and psychic life, examining in detail the alleged innate sinfulness through the concept of "cruelty." Exerting a strong influence here is the discourse of criminal anthropology, which at the turn of the century proffers in a flood of publications what is basically a "scientific construction of the 'evil child.'"[31] Setting the tone is the Turin physician Cesare Lombroso, who, taking a Social Darwinist approach, describes the born criminal. In his much-read work *Criminal Man* from 1876, the theorist of degeneration proceeds from the assumption that the criminal has remained in an earlier stage of human evolution and his behavior therefore resembles that of a primitive. On the seemingly irrefutable foundations of exact science he thus aims to explain that, considered *biologically*, the child is the epitome of all wicked qualities—an uncivilized creature characterized by innate asociality, amorality, conscienceless violence, and uninhibited lustfulness. It is above all the merciless cruelty of a child through which the spawning of evil seems to manifest:

> In general, the child prefers bad to good, He is more cruel than kind because he experiences strong emotions and has a sense of unlimited power. Thus we see him deriving great pleasure from breaking inanimate objects. He loves stabbing animals, drowning flies, hitting his dog, suffocating sparrows. Sometimes children dip cockroaches in hot wax and make them into kites or dress them as soldiers, prolonging their agony for months on end.[32]

The scene of the child tormenting animals recurs frequently in the scientific texts of the time. A genuine topos, it pervades not only the publications of criminologists and psychiatrists,[33] but also those of empirical development psychologists. The pioneers of this new discipline—for instance Stanley Hall, Karl Groos, William Stern, James Sully, and Karl Bühler—assign an important role to what they see as the unbridled destructive urge, the lust to kill, and indulge in torture. These texts also rely on a moral judgment, repeatedly criminalizing the savage acts of the child.[34] A work attracting relatively little attention by the German child psychologist Gustav Siegert, published in 1889 under the title *Problematische Kindesnaturen* (*Problematic Children*) characterizes through the study of a ten-year-old girl the epochal demystification of the divine child, now flaunting nothing less than a devilish visage:

> Whenever I met this child I was always strangely surprised to the same degree by the quaintness of her appearance. Like a rosebud only just unfurling, she appeared to be woven fully out of radiance and fragrance. [...] If I was poet I would be bold enough to call the child an embodied ray of moonshine. And yet, at times, a grating dissonance sounded out from this angelic child temper. With the very same serene facial expression that adorned her so quaintly,

in a sudden contrast to the respective fundamental mood the girl inflicted the most horrific cruelties on both her playmates and animals. For hours on end she was able to torture a fly, a beetle with a zeal, with a devotion worthy of far better things, and to revel in the convulsions of the crippled or perishing creature. Ruthlessly mistreating the house cat, the mother's cute lap dog seemed to be her greatest pleasure [...]. But while the girl could inflict a terrible callousness herself or watch others do such deeds, it burst into impassioned tears when told about an ill child, unfortunate beggars, or the cruel acts committed by others.[35]

Siegert's description of the anonymous girl still reveals all the bewilderment that merges with a large dose of helplessness as to how to explain the discrepancies and dissonances which come to light with the new sciences of the child in the second half of the nineteenth century. It is as if the literary transfiguration of the angelic creature following the Romantic model is vehemently contradicted. This is, however, merely a superficial discursive rivalry between science and poetry, for with their disillusioning of the child even child psychologists are still drawing on a Christian model, one that structures the conventional moral value judgments, as the title given to the considerations on the ten-year-old girl in the second chapter clearly highlights: "Angel or Devil?". It would seem that this question, posed by a whole epoch, is not easy to answer, for the sudden change from good to bad and from bad to good is something Siegert cannot explain. And so the chapter ends in pronounced indecision:

Almost despite oneself, the question remains: where does this strange mixture of angelic allurement and vampire-like perfidy come from? Which whim of the dark sorceress nature has created

> this human creature so queerly out of an angel's graceful sweet-
> ness and the devil's grin?[36]

The question is left open at the conclusion of the characteristic description of the ten-year-old girl. But as the text can
show, the period around 1900 is marked by the persistence
of Christian notions of childhood, which now emerge fully
in their irresolvable ambivalence. As in Siegert the logic of
"either-or" is ultimately superseded by the observation that
allows the child to appear as an odd mixture of contrary ideas,
in Modernism it is precisely the indistinguishability between
angel and devil, at once enigmatic and disturbing, that comes
to the fore.

## V.

Literary Modernism's ambivalent view of the child is not ade-
quately explained however by referring to the persistence of
Christian-bourgeois moral ideas if at the same time the discursive potency of Freudian psychoanalysis is ignored, its
eminent interest in early childhood needing to be considered
in the context of the turn of the century. Like his colleagues
in developmental psychology, Freud pointedly desists from
following the Romantic idealization, a clear distinction from
his contemporary progressive pedagogues, as he sets about
examining the experiences of early childhood relationships,
identifying in them a universal form of human sex life and
which he primarily studies with a view to their consequences for later psychological developments. In the context of
his considerations on infantile sexuality, Freud already refers early on to the destructive side of child nature, which

he also conceptualizes under the term "cruelty."[37] As a poly-morphous-perverse being, the child appears to be capable of every possible act of transgression imaginable, observable in the sadistic pleasure taken in mistreating small animals and playmates, which Freud attempts to explain with the early activation of the erogenous zones in the *Three Essays*, and then later in *Beyond the Pleasure Principle* from 1920 by assuming a death drive. In stark contrast to the Romantic discourse, the child is not at one with itself, but deeply split, riven by the non-homogenous paths forged by its savage desire.

As much as contemporaries felt that the studies of psycho-analysis on infantile sexuality broke a taboo, it needs to be kept in mind that almost all the elements of Freud's theory were already well known. What is new is probably the tone rather than the discussion itself.[38] The originality of the language Freud used in his texts lies in how it soberly de-moralizes the bourgeois discourse on childhood. In contrast to the crimi-nal anthropologists, development psychologists, and sexual pathologists of his time, Freud refrains from denouncing the child as being in anyway evil or wicked because of its sexual-ity or aggressive disposition. And perhaps this is precisely where the bone of contention lies, for psychoanalysis speaks, beyond sacralization and demonization, neither of angels or devils and sins. It is no coincidence that psychoanalysis con-ceptualizes the child through the prototype of material Freud, turning away from the Christian tradition, takes from the cul-tural reference system of Greek Antiquity, namely the story of Oedipus. The life of a child is thus not an idyll but a genuine tragedy, one that tells of the incestuous love of the mother and the murderous hate of the father. With this composite, as irre-solvable as it is antagonistic, of affection and rebellion, of love and hate, of erotic desire and the lust to kill, Freud takes into account the ambivalences of the child and with it the abysses of the bourgeois nuclear family—and precisely at just that historical juncture when the "cultural hegemony of Christianity" is beginning to buckle.[39] Wherever literary Modernism then springs to the defense of the child, it exposes the adults to be the leading practitioners of a language of appropriation and accusation. The father in Kafka's early short story *The Judgment* from 1913 condemns his son with the fatal words: "An innocent child, yes, that you were, truly, but still more truly have you been a devilish human being!"[40]

# Notes

## Introduction

1. See Hugh Cunningham, *The Invention of Childhood* (London: BBC Books, 2006); Heike Deckert-Peaceman, Cornelie Dietrich, and Ursula Stenger, eds., *Einführung in die Kindheitsforschung* (Darmstadt: WBG, 2010), pp. 22–31. For the controversial discussion on the "end of childhood," see Neil Postman, *The Disappearance of Childhood* (New York: Delacorte Press, 1982).

2. Philippe Ariès, *Centuries of Childhood: A Social History of Family Life*, trans. Robert Baldick (London: Pimlico, 1996).

3. For childhood in the Middle Ages, see Shulamith Shahar, *Childhood in the Middle Ages* (London: Routledge, 1990); James A. Schultz, *The Knowledge of Childhood in the German Middle Ages, 1100–1350* (Philadelphia: University of Pennsylvania Press, 1995); Albrecht Classen, ed., *Childhood in the Middle Ages and Renaissance* (Berlin and New York: Walter de Gruyter, 2005).

4. Ariès, *Centuries of Childhood*, p. 125: "In medieval society the idea of childhood did not exist; this is not to suggest that children were neglected, forsaken or despised. The idea of childhood is not to be confused with affection for children: it corresponds to an awareness of the particular nature of childhood, that particular nature which distinguishes the child from the adult, even the young adult. In medieval society, this awareness was lacking. That is why, as soon as the child could live without the constant solicitude of his mother, his nanny or his cradle-rocker, he belonged to adult society."

5. See Edward Shorter, *The Making of the Modern Family* (New York: Collins, 1975).

6. See Meike Sophia Baader, Florian Eßer, and Wolfgang Schröer, eds., *Kindheiten in der Moderne. Eine Geschichte der Sorge* (Frankfurt am Main and New York: Campus Verlag, 2014).

7. Hans-Heino Ewers, *Kindheit als poetische Daseinsform. Studien zur Entstehung der romantischen Kindheitsutopie im 18. Jahrhundert. Herder, Jean Paul, Novalis, Tieck* (Munich: Fink, 1989), p. 13.

8. Franz-Xaver Kaufmann, "Kinder als Außenseiter der Gesellschaft," *Merkur. Zeitschrift für europäisches Denken* 34, no. 8 (1980): pp. 761–771, esp. pp. 763, 767.

9.  Jean-Jacques Rousseau, *Emile, or On Education*, trans. Barbara Foxley (New York: E.P. Dutton, 1911), pp. 3, 54.

10. Niklas Luhmann, "Das Kind als Medium der Erziehung," in Niklas Luhmann, *Schriften zur Pädagogik*, ed. Dieter Lenzen (Frankfurt am Main: Suhrkamp, 2004), pp. 159–186, here p. 166.

11. Ibid., pp. 166, 169.

12. Friedrich Schiller, *Naïve and Sentimental Poetry, and On the Sublime: Two Essays*, trans. Julius A. Elias (New York: Ungar Publishing, 1984), p. 87.

13. Ellen Key, *The Century of the Child* (New York and London: G. P. Putnam's and Sons, 1909).

14. William Clarke Hall, *The State and the Child* (London: Friedrich A. Stokes Company, 1917), p. XI.

15. See for example, Hugh Cunningham, *Children and Childhood in Western Society Since 1500* (London and New York: Routledge, 2005), pp. 171–200; Meike Sophia Baader, "Die Kindheit der sozialen Bewegungen," in Baader, *Kindheiten in der Moderne*, pp. 154–189.

16. See Peter Gstettner, *Die Eroberung des Kindes durch die Wissenschaft. Aus der Geschichte der Disziplinierung* (Reinbek bei Hamburg: Rowohlt, 1981); Elisabeth Wiesbauer, *Das Kind als Objekt der Wissenschaft. Medizinische und psychologische Kinderforschung an der Universität Wien, 1800–1914* (Vienna and Munich: Löcker, 1982); for the child study movement, see Alice Boardman Smuts, *Science in the Service of Children, 1893–1935* (New Haven and London: Yale University Press, 2008); Marc Depaepe, *Zum Wohl des Kindes? Pädologie, pädagogische Psychologie und experimentelle Pädagogik in Europa und den USA, 1890–1940* (Weinheim: Deutscher Studien Verlag, 1993).

17. See Nicolas Pethes, *Zöglinge der Natur. Der literarische Menschenversuch des 18. Jahrhunderts* (Göttingen: Wallstein, 2007).

18. See Florian Eßer, "Die verwissenschaftlichte Kindheit," in Baader, *Kindheiten in der Moderne*, pp. 124–154; Felix Rietmann et al., "Knowledge of Childhood. Materiality, text, and the history of science – an interdisciplinary roundtable discussion," *British Journal for the History of Science* 50 (2017): pp. 111–141.

19. See the excellent study by Barbara Wittmann, *Bedeutungsvolle Kritzeleien. Eine Kultur- und Wissensgeschichte der Kinderzeichnung, 1500–1950* (Berlin and Zurich: Diaphanes, 2018).

20. Nicola Gess, *Primitives Denken. Wilde Kinder und Wahnsinnige in der literarischen Moderne (Müller, Musil, Benn, Benjamin)* (Munich: Fink, 2013), p. 77.

21. See André Turmel, "Das normale Kind. Zwischen Kategorisierung, Statistik und Entwicklung," in *Ganz normale Kinder. Heterogenität und Standardisierung kindlicher Entwicklung*, ed. Helga Kelle and Anja Tervooren (Weinheim: Juventa, 2008), pp. 17–40; and *A Historical Sociology of Childhood: Developmental Thinking, Categorization, and Graphic Visualization* (Cambridge: Cambridge University Press, 2008).

22. Wolfgang Rose, Petra Fuchs and Thomas Beddies, *Diagnose "Psychopathie". Die urbane Moderne und das "schwierige Kind". Berlin 1918–1933* (Vienna: Böhlau, 2016); for the history of child psychiatry, see Alexander von Gontard, "The Development of Child Psychiatry in Nineteenth Century Britain," *Journal of Child Psychology and Psychiatry* 29 (1988): pp. 569–588; Michael Neve and Trevor Turner, "History of Child and Adolescent Psychiatry," in *Child and Adolescent Psychiatry*, ed. Michael Rutter and Eric Taylor (Oxford: Wiley, 2002), pp. 382–395.

23. Cesare Lombroso, *Criminal Man*, trans. Mary Gibson and Nicole Hahn Rafter (Durham NC and London: Duke University Press, 2006), p. 163.

24. Sigmund Freud, *The Standard Edition of the Complete Psychological Works of Sigmund Freud, Volume VII (1901–1905): A Case of Hysteria, Three Essays on Sexuality and Other Works*, trans. James Strachey (London: Vintage, 2001), p. 191.

25. Albrecht Koschorke, *The Holy Family and its Legacy. Religious Imagination from the Gospels to Star Wars,* trans. Thomas Dunlap (New York: Columbia University Press, 2003), p. 171.

26. Ibid.

27. See Dieter Lenzen, "Kulturgeschichte der Vaterschaft," in *Wann ist der Mann ein Mann? Zur Geschichte der Männlichkeit*, ed. Walter Erhart and Britta Herrmann (Stuttgart and Weimar: Metzler, 1997), pp. 87–113; Dieter Thomä, *Väter. Eine moderne Heldengeschichte* (Munich: Hanser, 2008), pp. 173–177.

28. Walter Benjamin, "Old Toys," in *Selected Writings, vol. 2, Part 1, 1927–1930*, ed. Michael W. Jennings, Howard Eiland, Gary Smith, trans. Rodney Livingstone and others (Cambridge MA and London: Harvard University Press, 2005), p. 101.

29. Ibid.

30. Davide Giuriato, *Mikrographien. Zu einer Poetologie des Schreibens in Walter Benjamins Kindheitserinnerungen (1932–1939)* (Munich: Fink, 2006), p. 17.

31. Freud, *Standard Edition, vol. VII,* p. 176.
32. See George Boas, *The Cult of Childhood* (London: Warburg Institute, 1966).
33. See the pertinent study by Sally Shuttleworth, *The Mind of the Child. Child Development in Literature, Science and Medicine, 1840–1900* (Oxford: Oxford University Press, 2010).
34. See Chris Jenks, *Childhood* (London and New York: Routledge, 1996).
35. Dieter Richter, *Das fremde Kind. Zur Entstehung der Kindheitsbilder des bürgerlichen Zeitalters* (Frankfurt am Main: Fischer, 1987), p. 25.

## Idylls of Childhood (*Hoffmann—Stifter*)

1. Johann Gottfried Herder, "The Idyll," in *The Ladies' Magazine*, ed. Sarah Hale, trans. J. N. Nichols (Boston: Putnam & Hunt, 1829), p. 423.
2. Schiller, *On Naïve and Sentimental Poetry*, p. 103.
3. Jean Paul, *Horn of Oberon. Jean Paul Richter's School for Aesthetics*, trans. Margaret Hale (Detroit: Wayne State University Press, 1973), p. 187.
4. See Renate Böschenstein, "Idyllisch/Idylle," in *Ästhetische Grundbegriffe*, ed. Karlheinz Barck, Martin Fontius, and Dieter Schlenstedt (Stuttgart: Metzler, 2010), vol. 3, pp. 119–137, here p. 125.
5. See Tatjana Michaelis, *Der romantische Kindheitsmythos. Kindheitsdarstellungen der französischen Literatur von Rousseau bis zum Ende der Romantik* (Frankfurt am Main: Lang, 1986), pp. 63–84; on the desire of bourgeois culture for purity in relation to the genre of the fairytale, which is subject to a desexualizing comparable to the idyll, see Albrecht Koschorke, "Kindermärchen. Liminalität in der Biedermeierfamilie," in Albrecht Koschorke et al., *Vor der Familie. Grenzbedingungen einer modernen Institution* (Munich: Konstanz University Press, 2010), pp. 139–171.
6. Novalis, *Philosophical Writings*, trans. Margaret Mahony Stoljar (Albany: State University of New York Press, 1997), p. 41.
7. For the discursive production of child innocence in bourgeois culture, see Ariès, *Childhood*, pp. 98–124; see also Gert Ueding, "Verstoßen in ein fremdes Land. Kinderbilder der deutschen Literatur," *Neue Sammlung* 17 (1977): pp. 344–356.
8. Friedrich Fröbel, "Entwurf eines Planes zur Begründung und Ausführung eines KINDER-GARTENS [1840]," in Friedrich Fröbel, *Ausgewählte Schriften, vol. 1, Kleine Schriften und Briefe von 1809–1851*,

ed. Erika Hoffmann (Godesberg: Küpper, 1951), pp. 114–125, here p. 118. The extent of Fröbel's orientation on the Romantic idea of a paradisiacal childhood when modelling the new institution is also revealed by a work of his pupil Lina Morgenstern, *Das Paradies der Kindheit, Eine ausführliche Anleitung für Mütter und Erzieherinnen zur Kindespflege und Erziehung in den ersten sechs Jahren und zur praktischen Anwendung von Friedrich Fröbel's Spielbeschäftigungen in Haus und Kindergarten [1861]* (Vienna: Bichler, 1889).

9. Fröbel then directs attention to the child's active drive to form and create, emphasizing that everything needs to be excluded from the institution which could damage the natural development of the offspring: "The grand aim of the undertaking, the final, the overall purpose of the whole endeavor is: to educate humans early through doing, feeling, and thinking, fully appropriate to their character and circumstances, to human nature, and thus to the genuinely divine aptitude, and so furthermore to an all-round aptitude for life, through the true tending of childhood life, of childhood activity, through developing and shaping, through forming and directly living the child's pure essence. For this reason, anything that disturbs or indeed even destroys such an education [*Bildung*] is not to be tolerated anywhere in such an enterprise; on the contrary, it must seek to incorporate whatever fosters it. This is why there cannot be anything which would be useless and meaningless in the entire enclosure, including the outdoor area." Fröbel, "Entwurf eines Planes," pp. 119–120. For the tradition of the pedagogical garden, see Michael Niedermeier, "Nützlichkeit und Mysterien der Mutter Natur. Pädagogische Gärten der Philanthropen," in *Der imaginierte Garten*, ed. Günter Oesterle and Harald Tausch (Göttingen: Vandenhoeck & Ruprecht, 2001), pp. 157–197.

10. Michel Foucault, *Mental Illness and Psychology*, trans. Alan Sheridan (Berkley: University of California Press, 1997), pp. 80–81.

11. Gundel Mattenklott, "Phantastische Ländchen. Beiträge zu einem historisch-literarischen Atlas der Kindheit," in *Topographien der Kindheit. Literarische, mediale und interdisziplinäre Perspektiven auf Orts- und Raumkonstruktionen*, ed. Caroline Roeder (Bielefeld: transcript, 2013), pp. 301–312, here p. 301.

12. E.T.A. Hoffmann, *The Strange Child*, trans. Anthea Bell (London: Pushkin Press, 2010), pp. 129–130: "Christlieb, who was used to following Felix's example in everything, did the same with her own bag of sweets. This was too much for Sir Thaddeus. 'My most honored,

my noble cousin,' he cried, 'I beg you to make allowances for my poor simple boy's foolishness, but it's a fact that here in the country, living in such straitened circumstances ... I mean to say, how can anyone here bring up such nicely mannered children as yours?' Count Cyprianus smiled in a self-satisfied and extremely distinguished way as he looked at Hermann and Adelgunde. They had long finished their biscuits, and were sitting perfectly still on their chairs without moving a muscle and without any expression on their faces. The plump lady was smiling too as she said: 'Ah, my dear cousin, the education of our dear children is closer to our hearts than anything else.'"

13. See ibid., p. 144: "'Oh, we're so clumsy, we don't know any natural sciences!' And Christlieb began sobbing pitifully and shedding tears. Felix joined in, and both children wailed and cried, 'Poor children that we are, we don't know any natural sciences!'"

14. See ibid., p. 172: "When the children still made no move, Lady von Brakel was vexed and said, 'Good gracious me, children, what's all this? Master Inkblot will think you are very rude, uncouth peasant children. Come along, shake hands with your tutor.' The children steeled themselves to do as their mother told them, but when Master Inkblot took their hands they shrank away, screaming, 'Ow! Ouch!' The tutor laughed out loud and showed a needle that he was holding hidden in his hand on purpose to prick the children when they shook hands. [...] 'What was the idea of that, sir?' asked Sir Thaddeus von Brakel, rather put out. 'Oh, just my little joke,' replied Master Inkblot, 'and I can't seem to rid myself of the habit.'" See Dieter Richter's pertinent remarks on the link between Master Inkblot's needle and the reformist considerations on the ideal school desk at the end of the eighteenth century, in Richter, *Das fremde Kind*, pp. 274–275.

15. Hoffmann, *The Strange Child*, pp. 144–145.

16. This is underlined by how the strange child cannot be assigned a definitive sex: "So Felix thought the strange child was a boy, and Christlieb insisted that their new friend was a girl, and they could not agree." Ibid., p. 155.

17. Richter, *Das fremde Kind*, p. 278.

18. Hoffmann, *The Strange Child*, p. 168.

19. Ibid., p. 197. For the role of the dream between wish, truth, and illusion in the work of E.T.A. Hoffmann, see Gerhard Neumann, "Puppe und Automate. Inszenierte Kindheit in E.T.A. Hoffmanns Sozialisationsmärchen Nußknacker und Mausekönig," in *Jugend – ein*

*romantisches Konzept?*, ed. Günter Oesterle (Würzburg: Königshausen & Neumann, 1997), pp. 135–160.

20. See Rüdiger Steinlein, "Das fremde Kind – Maternalität, Kindlichkeit und Phantasie. Das Märchen als antipädagogischer Diskurs," in *Die domestizierte Phantasie. Studien zur Kinderliteratur, Kinderlektüre und Literaturpädagogik des 18. und frühen 19. Jahrhunderts* ed. Rüdiger Steinlein (Heidelberg: Winter, 1987), pp. 236–242.

21. This is the thesis of Detlef Kremer, "Idyll und Trauma. Kindheit in der Romantik," *E.T.A. Hoffmann Jahrbuch* 11 (2003): pp. 7–18, here p. 18.

22. Adalbert Stifter, *Werke und Briefe. Historisch-kritische Gesamtausgabe*, ed. Alfred Doppler and Wolfgang Frühwald, since 2001 by Alfred Doppler and Hartmut Laufhütte (Stuttgart: Kohlhammer, 1978ff), vol. 2.1., p. 16.

23. Ibid., vol. 2.2., p. 243.

24. See Jens Tismar, *Gestörte Idyllen. Über Jean Paul, Adalbert Stifter, Robert Walser und Thomas Bernhard* (Munich: Hanser, 1973), pp. 43–70. The conflict between nature and culture in Stifter's story is emphasized by Christian Begemann, *Die Welt der Zeichen. Stifter-Lektüren* (Stuttgart: Metzler, 1995) and Stefani Kugler, "Katastrophale Ordnung. Natur und Kultur in Adalbert Stifters Erzählung Kazensilber," in *Poetische Ordnungen. Zur Erzählprosa des deutschen Realismus*, ed. Ulrich Kittstein and Stefani Kugler (Würzburg: Königshausen & Neumann, 2007), pp. 121–141.

25. See Christine Oertel Sjörgen, "Myths and Metaphors in Stifter's Katzensilber," *The Journal of English and Germanic Philology* 86 (1987): pp. 358–371, here p. 371: "The shimmer of Katzensilber [...] reminds us that the reality of the reconstructed idyllic childhood here rests on an illusion, a splendid illusion."

26. Koschorke, "Kindermärchen," p. 171.

27. Stifter, *Werke und Briefe*, vol. 2.2., p. 246.

28. Albrecht Koschorke, "Erziehung zum Freitod. Adalbert Stifters pädagogischer Realismus," in *Die Dinge und die Zeichen. Dimensionen des Realistischen in der Erzählliteratur des 19. Jahrhunderts*, ed. Sabine Schneider and Barbara Hunfeld (Würzburg: Königshausen & Neumann, 2008), pp. 319–332.

29. Stifter, *Werke und Briefe*, vol. 2.2., p. 258.

30. For Stifter's reflections on childhood, see Davide Giuriato, "Kindheit," in *Stifter-Handbuch. Leben – Werk – Wirkung*, ed. Christian Begemann and Davide Giuriato (Stuttgart: Metzler, 2017), pp. 342–345.

31. Stifter, *Werke und Briefe*, vol. 2.4., p. 179. For more on the mysteriousness of the brown girl, see Michael Gamper, "Wetterrätsel. Zu Adalbert Stifters *Kazensilber*," in *Literatur und Nicht-Wissen. Historische Konstellationen 1730–1930*, ed. Michael Bies and Michael Gamper (Zurich: Diaphanes, 2012), pp. 325–338. In terms of literary history, the connection between the brown girl and Goethe's Mignon is discussed by Gunter H. Hertling, "Mignons Schwestern im Erzählwerk Adalbert Stifters *Katzensilber, Der Waldbrunnen, Die Narrenburg*," in *Goethes Mignon und ihre Schwestern. Interpretationen und Rezeption*, ed. Gerhart Hoffmeister (New York: Lang, 1993), pp. 165–197.

32. Stifter, *Werke und Briefe*, vol. 2.2., p. 274.

33. Ibid., p. 311.

34. The brown girl's acts of rescue are not described by the narrator but the grandmother: "It is a miracle how God awoke the thoughts in the head of the brown wild girl that she saw the clouds and brought the bundles across." Ibid., p. 276.

35. It is patently clear that the story also relates, following a topical metaphor, the fire catching alight in the farmyard to the outbreak of the passions in puberty, the proverbial fire of youth. Before he is saved by the brown girl, Sigismund is trapped in the corridor between the children's room and that of the grandmother: "From the children's room a door led to a corridor that went to the room of the grandmother. The door of the children's room snapped shut easily, and Sigismund, somewhat weak, could not open it. It was therefore probable that he had hurried from the children's room to the room of the grandmother to warn her, and behind him the door locked shut, only to find the room of the grandmother locked, that he wanted to get back into the children's room but couldn't, and was now trapped in the corridor." Ibid., pp. 300–301. And of course it stands out when the story again takes up with the same precision this exact description of the transitional position between the world of childhood, now lying in the past, and the world of adults, still in the future and thus barred. See ibid., pp. 305–306.

36. This refers back to the grandmother's first story on the "high Nußberg": she relates the story of the "brown farm girl" and how she disappeared after a farmer, at the behest of an anonymous voice from the woods, tells her that the "Rauh-Rinde is dead." Ibid., p. 248.

37. Beatrice Mall-Grob, *Fiktion des Anfangs. Literarische Kindheitsmodelle bei Jean Paul und Adalbert Stifter* (Stuttgart and Weimar: Metzler, 1999), p. 296.

38. See Eva Geulen, "Kinderlos," *Internationales Archiv für Sozialge-schichte der deutschen Literatur* 40, no. 2 (2015): pp. 420–440.

## Christmas

1.  It is surmised that this date was chosen because of its mythological roots in the ancient sun cult. See Wolfhart Pannenberg, "Mythos und Dogma im Weihnachtsfest," in *Das Fest*, ed. Walter Haug and Rainer Warning (Munich: Fink, 1989), pp. 57–58.

2.  See Ingeborg Weber-Kellermann, *Das Weihnachtsfest. Eine Kultur- und Sozialgeschichte der Weihnachtszeit* (Luzern and Frankfurt am Main: Bucher, 1978).

3.  For this term as distinct from "secularization," see Giorgio Agamben, *Profanations*, trans. Jeff Fort (New York: Zone Books, 2007), pp. 73–92.

4.  Friedrich Schleiermacher, *Christmas Eve Celebration. A Dialogue*, trans. Terrence N. Tice (Eugene: Cascade Books, 2010), p. 7.

5.  Ibid., p. 28.

6.  Koschorke, *The Holy Family*, p. 130.

7.  Schleiermacher, *Christmas Eve*, p. 33.

8.  Ibid., p. 63.

9.  Ibid., pp. 64–65.

10. Ibid., p. 70.

11. See for example Walter Jens, ed., *Es begibt sich aber zu der Zeit. Texte zur Weihnachtsgeschichte* (Frankfurt am Main: Fischer Klassik, 2012).

12. For an overview, see Claudia Öhlschläger, "Bergkristall," in Begemann and Giuriato, *Stifter-Handbuch. Leben – Werk – Wirkung*, pp. 83–87.

13. Adalbert Stifter, *Rock Crystal. A Christmas Tale*, trans. Elizabeth Mayer and Marianne Moore (New York: Pantheon Books, 1965), pp. 48 and 57.

14. Ibid., pp. 4–5 (emphasis mine).

15. See Begemann, *Die Welt der Zeichen*, p. 318.

16. Stifter, *Rock Crystal*, p. 84.

17. Ibid., p. 87. The passage in the original reads: "von dem Tage an erst recht das *Eigenthum* des Dorfes [...]." Stifter, *Werke und Briefe*, vol. 2.2., p. 239 (emphasis mine). The use of *Eigenthum*—"property" or

"possession"—underscores this, the children only now having the sense of belonging because they are considered chattels.

18. Stifter, *Rock Crystal*, p. 88: "But the children, sitting in the garden, can never forget the mountain, and earnestly fix their gaze upon it when, as in times past, the sun is out bright and warm, the linden diffuses its fragrance, the bees are humming, and the mountain looks down upon them as serene and blue as the sky above."

19. Sigmund Freud, *Standard Edition, vol. XVII*, p. 35.

## Rescuing Children (*Stifter*)

1. Moriz Enzinger, *Adalbert Stifter im Urteil seiner Zeit* (Vienna: Böhlau, 1968), pp. 88–90.

2. That the story points the way into "the very heart of Stifter's work" was already noted in the early article by Walter Rehm, "Stifters Erzählung *Der Waldgänger* als Dichtung der Reue," in Walter Rehm, *Begegnungen und Probleme. Studien zur deutschen Literaturgeschichte* (Bern: Francke, 1957), pp. 317–345, here p. 317.

3. For a survey, see Giuriato, "Kindheit."

4. For the history of the use of the back story, see Cornelia Zumbusch, "Nachgetragene Ursprünge. Vorgeschichten im Bildungsroman (Wieland, Goethe und Stifter)," *Poetica* 43, nos. 3–4 (2011): pp. 267–299.

5. In this sense Stifter's late autobiographical sketch *Mein Leben* (*My Life*) characterizes the period of childhood as a dark sphere prior to all distinctions—a "darkness of nothingness" ungraspable with concepts: "Far back in the empty void there is something like bliss and enchantment which pierced my inmost being with its fierce, almost annihilating power and which was unlike anything else in my future. The tangible signs which could be retained were these: there was a gleam, there was commotion, it was below. This must have been very early on, for it seems to me as if a vast darkness of nothingness lay all around this thing." Adalbert Stifter, *Tales of Old Vienna and other Prose*, trans. Alexander Stillmark (Riverside CA: Ariadne Press, 2016), p. 155.

6. See Lucien Malson et al., *Die wilden Kinder* (Frankfurt am Main: Suhrkamp, 1972); Harlan Lane, *The Wild Boy of Aveyron* (Cambridge MA: Harvard University Press, 1976); Julia Douthwaite, "Rewriting

the Savage: The Extraordinary Fictions of the Wild Girl of Champagne," *Eighteenth Century Studies* 28, no. 2 (1994/95): pp. 163–192.

7. See Stifter's considerations in *Persönliche Rechte*: "Only humans are persons. All that is beneath the human is a thing or an object [...]. But the human is a person at all times, and how does one recognize this personhood? The human is not a human at all times, for not at all times does the human have a free will. Up until a certain age children do not have a human will, but more like an animalistic appetite." Stifter, *Werke und Briefe*, vol. 8.2., p. 251.

8. As Nicolas Pethes notes, the very different stories of socialization *Tourmaline* and *Kazensilber*—when read in the context of pedagogic and scientific experiments on humans—are characterized precisely by the lack of any experimental result; see Pethes, *Zöglinge der Natur*, p. 386.

9. See Eva Geulen, *Worthörig wider Willen. Darstellungsproblematik und Sprachreflexion in der Prosa Adalbert Stifters* (Munich: ludicium, 1992), pp. 130–136; and Eva Geulen, "Adalbert Stifters Kinder-Kunst. Drei Fallstudien," *Deutsche Vierteljahresschrift für Literaturwissenschaft und Geistesgeschichte* 67 (1993): pp. 648–668.

10. See the review published in *Der Humorist* on November 27, 1846: "[*The Forest Wanderer*] is the story of a person [...], who lives thirteen years of the most blessed happiness, of the most heartfelt contentment with the woman of his soul, —and who both then freely separate because they remain childless! I find a certain unmoral principle of ingratitude in this idea [...]. Is there not more to marriage, nothing higher, nothing more spiritual than the urge to populate the world? Is marriage not a symbol of the divine world order [...]?" Quoted in Enzinger, *Adalbert Stifter im Urteil seiner Zeit*, p. 90.

11. See Michel Foucault, *The History of Sexuality. Volume I: An Introduction*, trans. Robert Hurley (London: Penguin, 1981), pp. 136–137 and p. 139: "[...] the right of the social body to ensure, maintain, or develop its life [...] a power that exerts a positive influence on life, that endeavors to administer, optimize, and multiply it, subjecting it to precise controls and comprehensive regulations." "The setting up, in the course of the classical age, of this great bipolar technology—anatomic and biological, individualizing and specifying, directed toward the performances of the body, with attention to the processes of life—characterized a power whose highest function was perhaps no longer to kill, but to invest life through and through."

12. Stifter, *Werke und Briefe*, vol. 8.2., p. 27.

13. Ibid., p. 125.

14. Ibid., vol. 3.1., pp. 120–121.

15. It is emphasized on several occasions that the boy is by no means exceptional: "He was no different than children usually are in forest regions, or rather, he was poorer than most of these children. Above his blue eyes sat a crop of blonde hair, just like, one could say, without exception, the children of such regions have." Ibid., pp. 121–122.

16. The final lines in *My Life* cite the passage from *The Forest Wanderer*: "From this window-sill I also saw what went on outside and I very often said: 'There's a man going to Schwarzbach, there's a woman going to Schwarzbach, there's a dog going to Schwarzbach, there's a goose going to Schwarzbach.' I also laid out pine kindling-wood lengthways, perhaps also binding them crosswise on this window-sill and said, 'I'm making Schwarzbach.'" Stifter, *Tales of Old Vienna*, pp. 157–158.

17. "It was strange that the boy now, since he'd actually been to the monastery down below, no longer built Hohenfurth, and no longer sent things on their way to Hohenfurth; was it now because he was older [...], or was it because he saw that, outside of Hohenfurth, the world still lies far away, and that it is not the end of things, or was it finally because the original image had stamped its presence in his mind in a very specific form, and has shooed away the indefinite aura of imagination [...]". Stifter, *Werke und Briefe*, vol. 3.1., pp. 125–126.

18. For the therapeutic promise of such a linguistically-mediated "instruction into the factual," see Albrecht Koschorke, "Das buchstabierte Panorama: Zu einer Passage in Stifters Erzählung *Granit*," *Vierteljahresschrift des Adalbert Stifter-Instituts* 38 (1989): pp. 3–13.

19. Stifter, *Werke und Briefe*, vol. 3.1., p. 133.

20. Fully in line with the philosophy of Leibniz and Wolff, education and enlightenment are a never-ending process towards an ideal goal for Stifter: "I have said, the best standpoint for humans would be that from where the clearest insight into all things and unswerving moral integrity is present; I have also said that this is a state that one cannot create immediately, but that it stands before our eyes as the ultimate goal, and that the task is to move ever closer to it. This state would be the most purely human". Ibid., vol. 8.2., p. 183.

21. Ibid., vol. 3.1., p. 133.

22. See ibid., vol. 8.2., p. 176: "Therefore we have to cultivate reason and free will, which are given to us only as seeds; there is no other path to achieve the happiness of humanity, because reason and free will are

given to humans alone as our supreme qualities, and because they, up to a point, which we are not yet even able to suspect, can be constantly developed."

23. See ibid., p. 120–121: "Besides the Church, the schools, the parishes, and the guilds, there is another corporation in the state that has an enormous influence on the education and improvement of humans, *the family*. [...] Man and woman enter a union in great love, they unify all their affairs, their possessions and aims. Out of this union children are born. [...] The family is therefore the pinnacle of parents and children, the most natural and intimate corporation on earth."

24. Ibid., vol. 3.1., p. 137.

25. Ibid., p. 138.

26. See Hermann Haefcke, *Handbuch des Abdeckereiwesens* [1906] (Oldenburg: Olms, 2006).

27. The knacker in Kleist's *Michael Kohlhaas* already plays a decisive role for self-understanding of the boundaries of culture, law, and state; see Davide Giuriato, "'Wolf der Wüste.' Michael Kohlhaas und die Rettung des Lebens," in *Ausnahmezustand der Literatur. Neue Lektüren zu Heinrich von Kleist*, ed. Nicolas Pethes (Göttingen: Wallstein, 2011), pp. 290–306.

28. See Foucault, *History of Sexuality*, vol. 1, p. 143.

29. "An entire lifetime earlier to what happened as we've described above, a little boy was born to parents far away from the hitherto locales, as five and sixty years later a boy was born to the gamekeepers. Both sets of parents had in common that after long years of unfruitful marriage they were now blessed with a child, for both the child born remained the only one, and with both it was secluded from a whole other world." Stifter, *Werke und Briefe*, vol. 3.1., p. 141.

30. Ibid., p. 145.

31. Ibid., p. 146.

32. Ibid., p. 151.

33. Ibid., p. 165.

34. Ibid., p. 166.

35. Ibid., pp. 186–188.

36. See Dirk Blasius, *Ehescheidung in Deutschland im 19. und 20. Jahrhundert* (Frankfurt am Main: Fischer, 1992), pp. 27–35.

37. See Günther Bernert and Hans Hattenhauer, eds., *Allgemeines Landrecht für die Preußischen Staaten von 1794* [1794] (Neuwied: Luchterhand, 1994), Zweyter Theil, Erster Titel, § 1.

38. Divorcing childless marriages is in fact possible given mutual consent since the *Allgemeines Preußisches Landrecht* (ibid., Zweyter Theil, Erster Titel, § 716: "Childless marriages can be divorced on the basis of mutual consent, provided that there is neither imprudence or hastiness, nor secret coercion from one or the other side to be feared."). This is not only based on the idea of a new contractual dispositional freedom of the individual, but also a population policy oriented on securing the welfare of the state. See Carl Heinz Ratschow et al., "Ehe/Eherecht/Ehescheidung," in *Theologische Realenzyklopädie*, ed. Gerhard Krause and Gerhard Müller (Berlin and New York: de Gruyter, 1982), vol. 9, pp. 308–311, p. 347.

39. See Ulrich Kinzel, *Ethische Projekte. Literatur und Selbstgestaltung im Kontext des Regierungsdenkens. Humboldt, Goethe, Stifter, Raabe* (Frankfurt am Main: Klostermann, 2000), pp. 356–359.

40. Wilhelm Heinrich Riehl, "The Family," in Wilhelm Heinrich Riehl, *The Natural History of the German People*, vol. 3, trans. David J. Diephouse (Lewiston, Queenston, Lampeter: Edwin Mellen Press, 1990), p. 299: "The idea of humanity can never be fully embodied by a single man or a single woman; it is only a married couple that constitutes a microcosm of humanity as a whole."

41. Ibid.

42. Ibid.

43. Lorenz von Stein, *System der Staatswissenschaft* (Stuttgart and Tübingen: Cotta, 1852), vol. 1, System der Statistik, der Populationistik und der Volkswirtschaftslehre, p. 94.

44. Albert Eberhard Friedrich Schäffle, *Bau und Leben des socialen Körpers: encyclopädischer Entwurf einer realen Anatomie, Physiologie und Psychologie der menschlichen Gesellschaft: mit besonderer Rücksicht auf die Volkswirthschaft als socialen Stoffwechsel* (Tübingen: Laupp, 1875–1878), vol. 3, p. 1 and p. 37.

45. For all the emphasis placed on the reproductive instinct, which concurrently had caused Malthus and his adherents to fear overpopulation, the moral freedom of the individual is by no means denied in the works of Riehl, von Stein, and Schäffle; instead, it is taken into consideration, albeit as a "component of the demographic dynamic." See Kinzel, *Ethische Projekte*, p. 358.

46. Stifter, *Werke und Briefe*, vol. 3.1., pp. 190–191.

47. See Sebastian Susteck, "Die Form der Fortpflanzung und die Form der Familie," in Koschorke, *Vor der Familie*, pp. 97–137.

48. This stems very much from the social function assigned to the woman in the nineteenth century and connects the female retreat into the private sphere with the task of conveying political practices and discourses. See Kinzel, *Ethische Projekte*, p. 363.

49. Stifter, *Werke und Briefe*, vol. 3.1., p. 201.

50. Ibid., p. 187.

51. See the seminal study by Johannes Lehmann, "Rettung bei Kleist," in Pethes, *Ausnahmezustand der Literatur*, pp. 249–269, esp. pp. 258–259; and Johannes Lehmann and Hubert Thüring, eds., *Rettung und Erlösung. Politisches Heil in der Moderne* (Munich: Fink, 2015).

52. Riehl, *The Family*, p. 306.

53. For the narrative "genre of children's misfortune" at the time of the historical transition from the premodern to the Enlightenment age, see Richter, *Das fremde Kind*, pp. 41–136; with reference to Stifter, see Cornelia Zumbusch, "Erzählen und Erziehen. Pädagogik der Zurückhaltung in Stifters *Mappe meines Urgroßvaters*," *Internationales Archiv für Sozialgeschichte der deutschen Literatur* 40, no. 2 (2015): pp. 479–502.

54. Stifter, *Rock Crystal*, p. 57.

## On the Threshold of Writing (*Rilke—Walser—Benjamin*)

1. See Marie-Luise Könneker, *Dr. Heinrich Hoffmanns 'Struwwelpeter.' Untersuchungen zur Entstehungs- und Funktionsgeschichte eines bürgerlichen Bilderbuches* (Stuttgart: Metzler, 1977).

2. Reimar Klein, *"Sieh einmal, hier steht er!" Struwwelpeters beschädigte Kinderwelt* (Frankfurt am Main: Insel, 2005), p. 10.

3. See Reinhard Kuhn, *Corruption in Paradise. The Child in Western Literature* (Hanover NH and London: University of New England Press, 1982); Yvonne-Patricia Alefeld, *Göttliche Kinder. Die Kindheitsideologie in der Romantik* (Paderborn: Schöningh, 1996); Ewers, *Kindheit als poetische Daseinsform*; Rosemary Lloyd, *The Land of Lost Content: Children and Childhood in Nineteenth-Century French Literature* (Oxford: Clarendon, 1992); Annette Simonis, *Kindheit in Romanen um 1800* (Bielefeld: Aisthesis, 1993), Meike Sophia Baader, *Die romantische Idee des Kindes und der Kindheit. Auf der Suche nach der verlorenen Unschuld* (Berlin: Luchterhand, 1996).

4. Heinrich Hoffman, *Slovenly Peter, or: Cheerful Stories and Funny Pictures for Good Little Folks,* trans. Mark Twain (Philadelphia: Porter and Coates, 1931), p. 8.

5. Ibid., p. 11.

6. See Katharina Rutschky, ed., *Schwarze Pädagogik. Quellen zur Naturgeschichte der bürgerlichen Erziehung* (Frankfurt am Main: Ullstein, 1977).

7. Michel Foucault, *Discipline and Punish. The Birth of the Prison*, trans. Alan Sheridan (London: Penguin, 1985), p. 183.

8. Quoted in Rutschky, *Schwarze Pädagogik,* p. 427.

9. Goethe's description of Mignon's lyrics already refers to the original brokenness of this childlike innocence, its uniqueness now beyond restoration: "The melody and the expression pleased Wilhelm greatly, though he could not make out all the words. So he asked her to repeat it, and explain it; then he wrote it down and translated it into German. He found, however, that he could not even approximate the originality of the phrases, *and the childlike innocence of the style was lost when the broken language was smoothed over and the disconnectedness removed.*" Johann Wolfgang Goethe, *Wilhelm Meister's Apprenticeship*, trans. Eric A. Blackall (Princeton: Princeton University Press, 1995), p. 83. (emphasis mine). See also Carolyn Steedman, *Strange Dislocations. Childhood and the Idea of Human Interiority (1780–1930)* (London: Virago, 1995).

10. See Barbara Wittmann, "Zeichnen, im Dunkeln. Psychophysiologie einer Kulturtechnik um 1900," in *Randgänge der Zeichnung*, ed. Werner Busch, Oliver Jehle, and Carolin Meister (Munich: Fink, 2007), pp. 165–186; and Barbara Wittmann, "Am Anfang. Theorien des Kritzelns im 19. Jahrhundert," in Friedrich Weltzien, ed., *Von selbst. Autopoietische Verfahren in der Ästhetik des 19. Jahrhunderts* (Bonn: Reimer, 2006), pp. 141–154.

11. See Jean-François Lyotard, *Lectures d'enfance* (Paris: Éditions Galilée, 1991), p. 39: "It is like birth and childhood, they are there before one is. [...] It is not I that is born, that comes into the world. I will be born later, with language, more accurately, when I leave childhood."

12. See Giorgio Agamben, "The Idea of Infancy," in Giorgio Agamben, *The Idea of Prose*, trans. Michael Sullivan and Sam Whitsitt (Albany: State University of New York Press, 1995), p. 97: "[...] children, not adults, entered language for the first time, and despite the forty millennia of the species homo sapiens, precisely the most human of his characteristics—the acquisition of language—has remained firmly

linked to an infantile condition and to an exteriority." See also Giorgio Agamben, *Infancy and History*, trans. Liz Heron (London: Verso, 2007), p. 55: "For the experience, the infancy at issue here, cannot merely be something which chronologically precedes language and which, at a certain point, ceases to exist in order to spill into speech. It is not a paradise which, at a certain moment, we leave for ever in order to speak; rather, it coexists in its origins with language—indeed, is itself constituted through the appropriation of it by language in each instance to produce the individual as subject."

13. Angelika Nix, *Das Kind des Jahrhunderts im Jahrhundert des Kindes. Zur Entstehung der phantastischen Erzählung in der schwedischen Kinderliteratur* (Freiburg im Breisgau: Rombach, 2002), p. 15.

14. Friedrich Nietzsche, "On the Future of Our Educational Institutions," in *The Complete Works of Friedrich Nietzsche, vol. 6, On the Future of Our Educational Institutions; Homer and Classical Philology*, ed. Oscar Levy, trans. J. M. Kennedy (New York: Russell & Russell, 1964), pp. 15–142.

15. Key, *The Century of the Child*, p. 139.

16. Ibid., p. 12.

17. Ibid., p. 46.

18. Ibid., p. 181. See also p. 5: "But he who knows that man has become what he now is under constant transformations, recognizes the possibility of so influencing his future development that a higher type of man will be produced. The human will is found to be a decisive factor in the production of the higher types in the world of animal and plant life. With what concerns our own race, the improvement of the type of man, the ennobling of the human race, the accidental still prevails in both exalted and lower forms. [...] In no respect has culture remained more backward than in those things which are decisive for the formation of a new and higher race of mankind." For Ellen Key's influence on the German reformist movement in general, see Bruno Schonig, "Reformpädagogik," in *Handbuch der deutsche Reformpädagogik 1880–1933*, ed. Diethart Kerbs and Jürgen Reulecke (Wuppertal: Hammer, 1998), pp. 319–330; for the pedagogic goals of the German youth movement, see Gottfried Küenzlen, *Der Neue Mensch. Eine Untersuchung zur säkularen Religionsgeschichte der Moderne* (Frankfurt am Main: Suhrkamp, 1997), pp. 153–173.

19. Key, *The Century of the Child*, p. 109.

20. Ibid., p. 190.

21. Ibid., p. 189.

22. Rainer Maria Rilke, *Sämtliche Werke, vol. 5*, publ. Rilke-Archiv, in cooperation with Ruth Sieber-Rilke and Ernst Zinn (Frankfurt am Main: Insel, 1965), p. 586.

23. Ibid., p. 13.

24. Ibid., p. 591.

25. See Rainer Maria Rilke and Ellen Key, *Briefwechsel*, ed. Theodore Fiedler (Frankfurt am Main: Suhrkamp, 1993); Rainer Maria Rilke, *Letters of Rainer Maria Rilke 1892–1910*, trans. Jane B. Greene and M. D. Herter Norton (New York: W. W. Norton & Company, 1945), pp. 96–234.

26. Rainer Maria Rilke, *The Notebooks of Malte Laurens Brigge: A Novel*, trans. Stephen Mitchell (New York: Vintage International, 1990), pp. 60–61.

27. See Friedrich A. Kittler, *Discourse Networks 1800/1900*, trans. Michael Metteer and Chris Cullens (Stanford: Stanford University Press, 1990), pp. 273–303.

28. As Rilke writes in a later letter from 1914 to Magda von Hattingberg: "Childhood—what actually was it? What *was* it, this childhood? Is there any other way of asking about except with this helpless question—what was it?" Quoted from Rainer Maria Rilke, *Letters on Life: New Prose Translations*, trans. Ulrich Baer (New York: The Modern Library, 2006), p. 67

29. This is the thesis elaborated by Ruth Hermann—without however any consideration of connections to the historical discourse—in her study *Im Zwischenraum zwischen Welt und Spielzeug. Eine Poetik der Kindheit bei Rilke* (Würzburg: Königshausen & Neumann, 2002): the unsayable childhood is positioned on the "margin" and, in the same move, at the center of Rilke's "poetic of figuration."

30. Rainer Maria Rilke, *Selected Works I: Prose*, trans. G. Craig Houston (London: The Hogarth Press, 1954), p. 40. Emphasis mine.

31. See Kittler, *Discourse Networks 1800/1900*, pp. 280–285.

32. Rainer Maria Rilke, *The Poetry of Rilke*, trans. Edward Snow (New York: North Point Press, 2009), p. 59.

33. For a survey, see Davide Giuriato, "Kindheit, Naivität, Dilettantismus," in *Robert Walser Handbuch. Leben – Werk – Wirkung*, ed. Lucas Marco Gisi (Stuttgart: Metzler, 2015), pp. 337–340. More recent studies embed Walser's poetics of childhood in the discursive context of a history of knowledge: Gwendolyn Whittaker, Überbürdung – Subversion – Ermächtigung. *Die Schule und die literarische Moderne, 1880–*

*1918* (Göttingen: V&R unipress, 2013) and Mareike Schildmann, *Poetik der Kindheit. Literatur und Wissen bei Robert Walser* (Göttingen: Wallstein, 2019).

34. See Hendrik Stiemer, *Über scheinbar naive und dilettantische Dichtung. Text- und Kontextstudien zu Robert Walser* (Würzburg: Königshausen & Neumann, 2014).

35. As a later prose piece from 1927 relates, Walser appears to have met Ellen Key during the winter of 1901–1902: "[...] and now I suddenly recall, sitting at the table and sketching this present sketch, Ellen Key, next to whom I once, that is umpteen years ago, years which have been so odd for humanity, sat while attending a dinner at the house of a Berlin publisher [...]. I would have mentioned a woman author whom I had met personally. Her books were read avidly by lots of people. This fighter for women's interests found a great echo with her writings at that time, or in other words, great success. [...] Be that as it may, at any rate I have mentioned for my pleasure an outstanding, meritorious woman." Robert Walser, *Sämtliche Werke*, ed. Jochen Greven (Frankfurt am Main: Suhrkamp, 1985–1986), vol. 19, pp. 127–129.

36. Robert Walser, "Fritz Kocher's Essays," in *A Schoolboy's Diary and Other Stories*, trans. Damion Searls (New York: New York Review of Books, 2013), pp. 17–18.

37. Walser, *Sämtliche Werke*, vol. 17, p. 179.

38. Wilhelm II, "Ansprache seiner Majestät des Kaisers und Königs," in *Verhandlungen über Fragen des höheren Unterrichts, Berlin 4. bis 17. Dezember* (Berlin: W. Hertz, 1891), pp. 70–76.

39. Walser, *A Schoolboy's Diary*, p. 34: "Only a bad essaywriter forgets to apply himself to the clarity of both the thoughts and the letters. You should always think first before you write. To start a sentence with an unfinished thought is sloppiness that can never be forgiven. And yet the slothful schoolboy believes that words will arise from other words. That is nothing but a vain and dangerous idea though. You get tired from walking on a country road much faster if you don't have a goal in mind.— Periods, commas, and other punctuation are a mistake to neglect, a mistake with a further consequence: untidiness of style. Style is a sense of order. Anyone with an unclear, untidy, unsightly mind will write in a style with those same qualities. From the style, says a proverb old and clichéd but no less true for all that, you can know the man." See Stephan Kammer, *Figurationen und Gesten des Schreibens. Zur Ästhetik der Produktion in Robert Walsers Prosa der Berner Zeit* (Tübingen: Max Niemeyer Verlag, 2003), pp. 84–89.

40. Walser, *A Schoolboy's Diary*, p. 17.

41. A 17-year-old girl tells of her experience in similar terms: "At first it was like facing a marvelous puzzle when I heard: 'choose your own topic'—and allow me an observation. Up until then I had just let my imagination do the work and forgotten about what is proximate, my surrounds. I was told to write in pretty, refined words, and now we're told: use the simplest and most natural words. [...] I had absolutely no idea what I should write about. And then suddenly—on a bright, joyous spring morning—the scales fell from my eyes. I had to fetch something before school and on this day met my first successful open-topic essay with my 'Morning Rider.'" Quoted from Otto Ludwig, *Der Schulaufsatz. Seine Geschichte in Deutschland* (Berlin: De Gruyter, 1988), p. 313.

42. See Klaus-Michael Hinz, "Wo die bösen Kinder wohnen. Robert Walsers Melancholie. Mit einer Fußnoten zu Kafkas Spielsachen," in *Robert Walser*, ed. Klaus-Michael Hinz and Thomas Horst (Frankfurt am Main: Suhrkamp, 1991), pp. 310–322.

43. Robert Walser, "The End of the World," in *Masquerade and Other Stories*, trans. Susan Bernofsky (Baltimore and London: The John Hopkins University Press, 1990), p. 101.

44. Robert Walser, *Aus dem Bleistiftgebiet*, ed. Bernhard Echte and Werner Morlang (Frankfurt am Main: Suhrkamp, 1985–2000). The complete edition, which by contrast will be the first to do justice to the material characteristics of this unique literary phenomenon, is still being compiled: Robert Walser, "Mikrogramme," in *Kritische Ausgabe*, ed. Wolfram Groddeck and Barbara von Reibnitz (Basel: Schwabe / Stroemfeld), sect. 6. Volumes published thus far are 6.1 (2016) and 6.2 (2019). Susan Bernofsky has translated a small selection of microscripts into English: Robert Walser, *Microscripts*, trans. Susan Bernofsky (New York: New Directions, 2010).

45. See the excellent overview by Stephan Kammer, "Das Phänomen Mikrographie," in Gisi, *Robert Walser Handbuch*, pp. 274–283.

46. Werner Morlang, "Melusines Hinterlassenschaft. Zur Demystifikation und Remystifikation von Robert Walsers Mikrographie," *Runa* 21 (1994): pp. 81–99, here pp. 91–92.

47. This figure from Jungian psychology (see Marie-Louise von Franz, *Der ewige Jüngling. Der Puer aeternus und der kreative Genius im Erwachsenen* [Munich: Kösel, 1987]) is drawn on by Christopher Middleton in "A Parenthesis to the Discussion of Robert Walser's Schizophrenia," in *Robert Walser Rediscovered. Stories, fairy-tale plays, and*

*critical responses*, ed. Mark Harman, ed (Hanover NH and London: University Press of New England, 1985), pp. 190–194.

48. Robert Walser, *Briefe*, ed. Jörg Schäfer with the assistance of Robert Mächler (Frankfurt am Main: Suhrkamp, 1979), pp. 300–301.

49. In a microscript draft transcribed by Walser and published under the title *Pencil Sketch*, the path from micrography into clean copy is described as entering into the definitiveness of the symbolic: "And if I may now offer something that concerns me personally, let me report that it occurred to me always first to commit my prose to paper in pencil before inking it into definitiveness as neatly as possible." Walser, *Microscripts*, p. 31.

50. See Schildmann, *Poetik der Kindheit*, p. 340.

51. Ibid., pp. 362–370.

52. Walser, *Aus dem Bleistiftgebiet*, vol. 4, p. 410.

53. See Christian Walt, *Improvisation und Interpretation. Robert Walsers Mikrogramme lesen* (Frankfurt am Main: Stroemfeld, 2015), pp. 45–48.

54. See for example Joachim Strelis, *Die verschwiegene Dichtung. Reden, Schweigen, Verstummen im Werk Robert Walsers* (Frankfurt am Main: Lang, 1991) and Kerstin von Schwerin, *Minima Aesthetica. Die Kunst des Verschwindens* (Frankfurt am Main: Lang, 2001).

55. Benjamin, *Selected Writings*, vol. 1, pp. 50–51; see Heinz Brüggemann, *Walter Benjamin. Über Spiel, Farbe und Phantasie* (Würzburg: Königshausen & Neumann, 2011).

56. Walter Benjamin Archiv, ed., *Walter Benjamins Archive. Bilder, Texte und Zeichen* (Frankfurt am Main: Suhrkamp, 2006), pp. 76–119.

57. Klaus Doderer, ed., *Walter Benjamin und die Kinderliteratur. Aspekte der Kinderkultur in den zwanziger Jahren* (Weinheim and Munich: Juventa, 1988).

58. Benjamin, *Selected Writings*, vol. 1, pp. 406–413; vol. 2, pp. 250–256, vol. 1, pp. 435–443; vol. 2, pp. 250–256.

59. Walter Benjamin, *Gesammelte Schriften*, ed. Rolf Tiedemann and Herrmann Schweppenhäuser (Frankfurt am Main: Suhrkamp, 1989), vol. 3, pp. 262–272, pp. 311–314; vol. 4.2, pp. 619–610.

60. Benjamin, *Selected Writings*, vol. 2, pp. 113–116; pp. 117–121; pp. 297–298; pp. 726–727.

61. Ibid., pp. 201–206.

62. Ibid., pp. 201–206; pp. 273–275; see Horst Bokma, *Das pädagogische Experiment des Schreibenden. Untersuchungen zu Walter Benjamins Rezensionen pädagogischer Literatur von 1924 bis 1932* (Frankfurt am Main: Lang, 2000) and Giulio Schiavoni, "Zum Kinde," in *Benjamin-*

*Handbuch. Leben – Werk – Wirkung*, ed. Burkhardt Lindner (Stuttgart: Metzler, 2011).

63. Benjamin, *Gesammelte Schriften*, vol. 4.1, pp. 113–116.
64. Ibid., vol. 4.2, pp. 674–695, pp. 316–346. See Jeffrey Mehlmann, *Walter Benjamin for Children. An Essay on his Radio Years* (Chicago: University of Chicago Press, 1993).
65. Benjamin, *Selected Writings*, vol. 2, pp. 595–637.
66. Ibid., vol. 3, pp. 344–423.
67. See Giuriato, *Mikrographien*.
68. Benjamin, *Selected Writings*, vol. 2, pp. 694–698 and pp. 720–722.
69. See Eva Geulen, "Legislating Education. Kant, Hegel, and Benjamin on Pedagogical Violence," *Cardozo Law Review* 26, no. 3 (2005): pp. 943–956.
70. Benjamin, *Selected Writings*, vol. 2, p. 101.
71. Ibid.
72. See for example Peter Schünemann, "Kindheitsmuseum Walter Benjamin," *Neue Rundschau* 103, no. 3 (1992): pp. 128–139.
73. Benjamin, *Selected Writings*, vol. 1, p. 449.
74. Ibid., p. 412.
75. Benjamin, *Gesammelte Schriften*, vol. III, p. 273.
76. Walter Benjamin, *The Correspondence of Walter Benjamin, 1910–1940*, trans. Manfred and Evelyn Jacobson (Chicago: University of Chicago Press, 1994), p. 269.
77. Benjamin, *Selected Writings*, vol. 1, pp. 449–450.
78. Susan Buck-Morss, *The Dialectics of Seeing: Walter Benjamin and the Arcades Project* (Cambridge MA: MIT Press, 1989), p. 265.
79. Marleen Stoessel, *Aura. Das vergessene Menschliche. Zu Sprache und Erfahrung bei Walter Benjamin* (Munich: Hanser, 1983), pp. 169–173.
80. See Gess, *Primitives Denken*, pp. 365–421.
81. Benjamin, *Selected Writings*, vol. 2, p. 285.
82. Gershom Scholem, *Walter Benjamin. The Story of a Friendship*, trans. Harry Zohn (New York: New York Review of Books, 2003), p. 57.
83. See Benjamin's criticism of the contemporary trend in toys: "If we survey the entire history of toys, it becomes evident that the question of size has far greater importance than might have been supposed. In the second half of the nineteenth century, when the long-term decline in these things begins, we see toys becoming larger, the unassuming, the tiny, and the playful all slowly disappear." *Selected Writings*, vol. 2, p. 114.

84. See Nicolas Pethes, "Die Arbeit am Mythos 'Kindheit' bei Walter Benjamin," in *Kindheit und Literatur. Konzepte – Poetik – Wissen*, ed. Davide Giuriato, Philipp Hubmann, and Mareike Schildmann (Freiburg im Breisgau: Rombach, 2018), pp. 57–73, esp. p. 67.

85. As Benjamin puts it in his review of Gomez de la Serna's *Le cirque* from 1927, when attending a circus, "the human being is a guest in the animal kingdom." *Gesammelte Schriften*, vol. 3, p. 72.

86. This is how the editors present the wording in Benjamin, *Gesammelte Schriften*, vol. 6, p. 200.

87. In *Berlin Childhood around 1900* Benjamin encapsulates this thought in "The Reading Box," where he describes learning to read and write—and points out that learning entails losing the ability to learn: "[...] I can dream of the way I once learned to walk. But that doesn't help. I now know how to walk; there is no more learning to walk." Benjamin, *Selected Writings*, vol. 3, p. 396.

88. Benjamin, *Gesammelte Schriften*, vol. 3, p. 311. Quoted from Esther Leslie, "Colonial and Capitalist Pedagogy," *Pedagogy, Culture & Society* 24, no. 4 (2016): p. 521.

89. Benjamin, *Gesammelte Schriften*, vol. 3, p. 269.

90. "At a stroke, the words throw in their costumes and in the twinkling of an eye they are caught up in a battle, love scenes, or a brawl. This is how children write their stories, but also how they read them. And there are rare, impassioned ABC-books that play a similar sort of game in pictures. [...] The genuine worth of such straightforward picture books is far removed from the rationalist crudeness that caused them to be recommended in the first place. [...] These carnivals overflow even into the more serious space of ABC-books and reading primers." Benjamin, *Selected Writings*, vol. 1, pp. 435–437.

91. Benjamin, *Gesammelte Schriften*, vol. 3, p. 272.

92. Ibid., p. 268.

93. Ibid., p. 314.

94. Ibid., p. 312.

95. Ibid., p. 314.

96. Ibid., vol. 2.1, p. 14. The reference to this important source is taken from an article by Eva Geulen, "Erziehungsakte," in *Rhetorik: Figuration und Performanz*, ed. Jürgen Fohrmann (Stuttgart and Weimar: Metzler, 2004), pp. 629–652, esp. p. 643.

97. Benjamin, *Gesammelte Schriften*, vol. 3, p. 314.

98. "Nothing against these old primers, but the 'seriousness of life' spoke out of them, and the finger that traveled along their lines had

crossed the threshold of a realm out of whose territory no wanderer returns." (Ibid.)

99.   Benjamin, *Selected Writings*, vol. 1, p. 80.

100. Giorgio Agamben, *The Time That Remains. A Commentary on the Letter to the Romans*, trans. Patricia Dailey (Stanford: Stanford University Press, 2005), p. 39.

101. William T. Preyer, *The Mind of the Child. Observations Concerning the Mental Development of the Human Being in the First Years of Life*, trans. H. W. Brown (New York: D. Appleton & Co., 1893), p. xv.

102. Key, *The Century of the Child*, p. 190.

103. Wittmann, "Zeichnen, im Dunkeln," p. 174.

104. See Juliane Prade, *Sprachoffenheit. Mensch, Tier und Kind in der Autobiographie* (Würzburg: Königshausen & Neumann, 2013).

105. Karl Bühler, *Die geistige Entwicklung des Kindes* (Jena: Fischer, 1918), p. 439. An English, however summarized, version can be found in Karl Bühler, *The Mental Development of the Child, a Summary of Modern Psychological Theory*, trans. Oscar Oeser (New York: Hartcourt, Brace & Co., 1930).

106. In the notes to his inaugural lecture at the University of Geneva in 1891, Ferdinand de Saussure, referring to the object of his research, expressly states that language is a formation "without age" and "without childhood": "To recapitulate the main points we have arrived at in these first hours, I would certainly insist on the radical impossibility of not merely a break but that of a leap in the continuous transmission of language since the first day, since a human society has spoken – on the various, instantly evidential points that no language can perish unless it is violently repressed; – that no [language] has an age and no [language] has a childhood, that finally no new language will ever be born under the sun [...]." Ferdinand de Saussure, *Linguistik und Semiologie: Notizen aus dem Nachlaß. Texte, Briefe und Dokumente* (Frankfurt am Main: Suhrkamp, 2003), p. 236.

## Becoming-Child (*Walser*)

1.    See the sentence in the text *Kindliche Rache*: "Sie erhielten ein Etwas, wovon sie sich glückstrahlend überzeugten, es sei ein Kind" / "They received a something of which they beamingly convinced themselves that it's a child." Walser, *Sämtliche Werke*, vol. 18, p. 298

2. Walser, *Aus dem Bleistiftgebiet*, 1985–2000, vol. 5, p. 231.

3. Ibid.

4. This is encapsulated in a prose piece published in 1925 in the collection *Die Rose* and entitled "Das Kind." The main character is introduced as a "child" of "meanwhile forty years." Walser, *Sämtliche Werke*, vol. 8, p. 75; as the plot unfolds, this child remains inscrutable to both himself and other: "I am one who doesn't exactly know what he actually is. [...] No one is entitled to behave towards me as if he knew me." Ibid., pp. 77–78.

5. Walser, *Aus dem Bleistiftgebiet*, vol. 4, pp. 38–41.

6. Ibid., p. 42.

7. Walser, *Sämtliche Werke*, vol. 20, p. 137. Significantly, Walser's text *Mutter und Kind* (*Mother and Child*) was first published in a special issue of the journal *Individualität* (which addressed the anthroposophy milieu) focusing on "the world of the child." *Individualität*, 4 (1929): pp. 120–121.

8. See Gess, *Primitives Denken*.

9. See the essay "Experience and Poverty" wherein, at about the same time, Benjamin develops a positive concept of the barbarian: "Barbarism? Yes, indeed. We say this in order to introduce a new, positive concept of barbarism. For what does poverty of experience do for the barbarian? It forces him to start from scratch; to make a new start; [...] Klee's figures [...] in their general expression [...] obey the laws of their interior. Their interior, rather than their inwardness; and this is what makes them barbaric. [...] for humanlikeness—a principle of humanism—is something they reject [...] The Russians, too, like to give their children 'dehumanized' names." Benjamin, *Selected Writings*, vol. 2, pp. 732–733. A poetological orientation of this concept of the barbarian is anticipated in Benjamin's description of Walser's "fascinating linguistic wilderness." Ibid., p. 257.

10. Jacob and Wilhelm Grimm, *Deutsches Wörterbuch* (Leipzig: Hirzel, 1854–1960), vol. 11, col. 707.

11. Walser, *Aus dem Bleistiftgebiet*, vol. 1, pp. 64–65. Written between May and July 1925, the draft is on microscript sheet 480 (fig. 6) with a series of other notes, which deal with the problem of plagiarism and the *mise-en-abîme* in art theory (ibid., pp. 57–59) and then followed by considerations on the child-like world of the fable and animals (ibid., pp. 79–81), of the lark and a talking cuckoo (ibid., pp. 133–134), a sketch on "being-new-at-a-place" (ibid., pp. 63–64), and a draft that can be read as a small fable on writing novels (ibid., pp. 115–118).

12. Grimm, *Deutsches Wörterbuch*, vol. 11, col. 55.
13. Friedrich Schiller, *On the Aesthetic Education of Man, in a Series of Letters*, trans. Reginald Snell (London: Routledge, 1954), p. 80.

## Little Hans (*Freud—Kafka*)

1. See Nicolas Pethes, "Vom Einzelfall zur Menschheit. Die Fallgeschichte als Medium der Wissenspopularisierung zwischen Recht, Medizin und Literatur," in *Popularisierung und Popularität*, ed. Gereon Blaseio, Hedwig Pompe, and Jens Ruchatz (Cologne: DuMont, 2005), pp. 63–92.
2. Foucault, *Discipline and Punish*, pp. 193–194.
3. Grimm, *Deutsches Wörterbuch*, vol. 10, col. 456.
4. Jacques Lacan, *La relation d'objet. Le Seminaire. Livre IV* (Paris: Seuil, 1998).
5. Freud, *Standard Edition, vol. X*, p. 5.
6. Lacan, *La relation d'objet*, p. 344.
7. See Barbara Wittmann, "'Drawing Cure,' Die Kinderzeichnung als Instrument der Psychoanalyse," in *Spuren erzeugen. Zeichnen und Schreiben als Verfahren der Selbstaufzeichnung*, ed. Barbara Wittmann (Berlin: Diaphanes, 2009), pp. 109–144.
8. Freud, *Standard Edition, vol. X*, p. 6.
9. Ibid., p. 5.
10. In a postscript from 1922 Freud reassures, recalling how at the time of publication many had predicted in great indignation "a most evil future [...] for the poor little boy, because he had been 'robbed of his innocence' at such a tender age and had been made the victim of a psychoanalysis," that Little Hans was now a strapping young man, free of any inhibitions or troubles, who could remember nothing about his treatment as a child. Ibid., p. 148.
11. Freud, *Standard Edition, vol. IX*, p. 135.
12. Freud, *Standard Edition, vol. X*, p. 7.
13. Ibid., p. 147.
14. See the pertinent study by Christoph Hoffmann, *Unter Beobachtung. Naturforschung in der Zeit der Sinnesapparate* (Göttingen: Wallstein, 2006).
15. Freud, *Standard Edition, vol. X*, p. 104: "It is true that during the analysis Hans had to be told many things that he could not say himself, that he had to be presented with thoughts which he had so far shown

no signs of possessing, and that his attention had to be turned in the direction from which his father was expecting something to come. This detracts from the evidential value of the analysis; but the procedure is the same in every case. For a psychoanalysis is not an impartial scientific investigation, but a therapeutic measure."

16. Ibid., p. 111.
17. Ibid., pp. 42–43.
18. Ibid., p. 15.
19. Freud, *Standard Edition, vol. VII*, p. 191.
20. Freud, *Standard Edition, vol. X*, pp. 48–49.
21. Ibid., p. 66.
22. Lacan, *La relation d'objet*, p. 349.
23. Freud, *Standard Edition, vol. X*, p. 95.
24. See Susanne Lüdemann, *Mythos und Selbstdarstellung. Zur Poetik der Psychoanalyse* (Freiburg im Breisgau: Rombach, 1994), esp. pp. 117–152.
25. Franz Kafka, *The Castle*, trans. Mark Harman (New York: Schocken Books, 1998), pp. 141–150.
26. Ibid., p. 116. For "questioning" and "interrogating" in general, see Michael Niehaus, *Das Verhör. Geschichte – Theorie – Fiktion* (Munich: Fink, 2003).
27. Ibid., p. 147.
28. Ibid., p. 158.
29. Ibid., pp. 142–143.
30. Ibid., pp. 143–144.
31. Ibid., p. 143: "Hans spoke of his father with reverence or fear, but only when there was no mention of his mother; when set against his mother, his father evidently counted for little; incidentally, no matter how you questioned him about his family life, he never responded […]."
32. Ibid., p. 148.
33. Ibid., p. 149.
34. For Kafka's skeptical relationship to psychoanalysis in general, see Peter-André Alt, *Franz Kafka. Der ewige Sohn* (Munich: C.H. Beck, 2005), pp. 308–312, and Thomas Anz, "Psychoanalyse," in *Kafka-Handbuch. Leben – Werk – Wirkung*, ed. Bernd Auerochs and Manfred Engel (Stuttgart: Metzler, 2010), pp. 65–72. The reconstruction of another case is also considered to play a role for the Hans chapter in *The Castle*: Otto Groß, whom Kafka knew personally, was forcibly admitted to an asylum by his father, the law professor Hans Groß, in

1915. See Malte Kleinwort, *Der späte Kafka – Spätstil als Stilsuspension* (Munich: Fink, 2013), who however does not follow up the obvious allusions to Freud's case of little Hans.

35. Franz Kafka, "The Judgment," in *The Complete Stories*, trans. Willa and Edwin Muir (New York: Schocken Books, 1971), p. 87; for Kafka's post-Romantic reflections on childhood, see Achim Geisenhanslüke, "Kafkas schmutzige Kinder. Schwellenerfahrungen in *Der Verschollene*," in *Liminale Anthropologien. Zwischenzeiten, Schwellenphänomene, Zwischenräume in Literatur und Philosophie*, ed. Jochen Achilles, Roland Borgards, and Brigitte Burrichter (Würzburg: Königshausen & Neumann, 2012), pp. 199–208.

36. See Gerhard Neumann, "Franz Kafka: Der Name, die Sprache und die Ordnung der Dinge," in *Franz Kafka: Schriftverkehr*, ed. Wolf Kittler and Gerhard Neumann (Freiburg im Breisgau: Rombach, 1990), pp. 11–29.

37. For Freud's accompanying narrative strategies, which with their authorial gestures link into the novella tradition of the nineteenth century, see Marcus Krause, "'Seelensucher'. Freuds *Bruchstück einer Hysterie-Analyse* als Versuchsanordnung zwischen Literatur und Wissenschaft," in *"Es ist ein Laboratorium, ein Laboratorium für Worte." Experiment und Literatur III, 1890–2010*, ed. Michael Bies and Michael Gamper (Göttingen: Wallstein, 2011), pp. 72–95.

38. Franz Kafka, *The Blue Octavo Notebooks*, ed. Max Brod, trans. Ernst Kaiser and Eithne Wilkins (New York: Schocken Books, 1954), pp. 76–77.

39. In his diary in 1916 Kafka notes another Hans story, the dream of an endangered childhood. See Franz Kafka, *The Diaries of Franz Kafka 1914–1922*, ed. Max Brod, trans. Martin Greenberg (New York: Schocken Books, 1949), pp. 148–152.

40. This intimate entwinement between *casus* and *lapsus* is pointedly expressed by the village mayor when he states that the "case" of K. has arisen because of a lapse on the part of the supervising authorities: "Are there control agencies? There are *only* supervising authorities. Of course they aren't meant to find errors, in the vulgar sense of the term, since no errors occur, and even if an error does occur, as in your *case*, who can finally say that it is an error," Kafka, *The Castle*, p. 65 (emphasis mine).

41. See Nicolas Pethes, *Literarische Fallgeschichten. Zur Poetik einer epistemischen Schreibweise* (Göttingen: Wallstein, 2016).

42. Susanne Lüdemann, "Literarische Fallgeschichten. Schillers *Verbrecher aus verlorener Ehre* und Kleists *Michael Kohlhaas*," in *Das Beispiel. Epistemologie des Exemplarischen*, ed. Jens Ruchatz, Stefan Willer, and Nicolas Pethes (Berlin: Kadmos, 2007), pp. 208–223, here p. 210.

## This Briefest Childhood (*Kafka*)

1. For a detailed philosophical discussion of the fragment B 52 in its "entwining of play, language, and world," see Alexander Aichele, *Philosophie als Spiel. Platon – Kant – Nietzsche* (Berlin: De Gruyter, 2000) pp. 15–36.

2. See the excellent overview by Enzo Degani, *Aion* (Bologna: Pàtron, 1957), pp. 35–54.

3. Conrad Lackeit, *Aion. Zeit und Ewigkeit in Sprache und Religion der Griechen* (Königsberg: Hartungsche Buchdruckerei, 1916), p. 41.

4. Ibid., p. 11.

5. Ulrich von Wilamowitz-Moellendorff, *Euripides Herakles* (Berlin: Weidmann, 1909), p. 364.

6. Kafka, *The Complete Stories*, p. 226.

7. Kafka visited Riva on Lake Garda twice in 1913. See *The Diaries of Franz Kafka 1910–1913*, ed. Max Brod, trans. Joseph Kresh (New York: Schocken Books, 1948), p. 278.

8. See the seminal studies by Hartmut Binder, "Der Jäger Gracchus. Zu Kafkas Schaffensweise und poetischer Topographie," *Jahrbuch der deutschen Schillergesellschaft* 15 (1971): pp. 375–440, and *Kafka: Der Schaffensprozeß* (Frankfurt am Main: Suhrkamp, 1983), pp. 191–270.

9. See Gerhard Neumann, "Die Arbeit im Alchimistengäßchen (1916–1917)," in *Kafka-Handbuch*, ed. Hartmut Binder (Stuttgart: Kröner, 1979), vol. 2, pp. 313–350, esp. pp. 336–339; and Rainer Nägele, "Auf der Suche nach dem verlorenen Paradies. Versuch einer Interpretation zu Kafkas *Der Jäger Gracchus*," *The German Quarterly* 47, no. 1 (1974): pp. 60–72.

10. Kafka, *The Complete Stories*, p. 226.

11. Franz Kafka, *Historisch-kritische Ausgabe sämtlicher Handschriften, Drucke und Typoskripte. Oxforder Oktavheft 1 & 2*, ed. Roland Reuß and Peter Staengle (Frankfurt am Main and Basel: Stroemfeld, 2006), pp. 10–11.

12. Franz Kafka, *Abandoned Fragments. Unedited Works 1897–1917*, trans. Ina Pfitzner (New York: Sun Vision Books, 2012), p. 164.

13. Ibid., p. 261.

14. Kafka, *The Complete Stories*, p. 228.

15. Ibid., p. 227.

16. For Kafka's experiments with "art as play" at the time of the *Country Doctor* collection (1917), see Gerhard Neumann, "Nachrichten vom Pontus. Das Problem der Kunst im Werk Franz Kafkas," in *Franz Kafka: Schriftverkehr*, ed. Wolf Kittler and Gerhard Neumann (Freiburg im Breisgau: Rombach, 1990), pp. 164–198. Following Neumann's differentiating of play, the dice played by the boys in Kafka's sketch would stand for an "autonomous play with language [...], for the language of art taking on its own momentum, as a speaking about language and language production." Ibid., p. 118.

17. See Kafka's diary entry of January 16, 1922: "The clocks are not in unison; the inner one runs crazily on at a devilish or demoniac or in any case inhuman pace; the outer one limps along at its usual speed. What else can happen but that the two worlds split apart, and they do split apart, or at least clash in a fearful manner." *The Diaries of Franz Kafka 1914–1923*, p. 202.

18. Kafka, *Abandoned Fragments*, p. 168.

19. See Annette Schütterle, *Franz Kafkas Oktavhefte: Ein Schreibprozeß als 'System des Teilbaues'* (Freiburg im Breisgau: Rombach, 2002), p. 108. For many years, *Hunter Gracchus*—first published by Max Brod under this title in Franz Kafka, *Beim Bau der Chinesischen Mauer* (Munich: Kiepenheuer, 1931), pp. 40–45—was edited as a continuous narrative with beginning and end. See for example Franz Kafka, *The Complete Stories*, pp. 226–230.

20. The problem of narrative consistency is itself addressed in the sketches: in Octavo Notebook D a conversation with Gracchus that opens with the words—"Gracchus, I have one request. First tell me briefly the whole story, how things stand with you"—breaks off a little later with the remark: "but now I'd like to know something about you, the whole story." Kafka, *Abandoned Fragments*, p. 204. The impossibility of coherently relating Gracchus's life is underlined by how Kafka interrupts the sketch with a dash in order to then continue with words which fail to form a complete sentence: "Ah, the whole story. The old, old stories." Ibid.

21. Ibid., p. 145.

22. "As man among men, Heraclitus was incredible; and though he was seen paying attention to the play of noisy children, even then he was reflecting upon what never man though of on such occasion: the play of the great world-child, Zeus. He had no need of men, not even for his discernments. [...] For the world needs truth eternally, therefore she needs also Heraclitus eternally." Friedrich Nietzsche, "Philosophy During the Tragic Age of the Greeks," in *The Complete Works of Friedrich Nietzsche, vol. 2, Early Greek Philosophy*, ed. Oscar Levy, trans. Maximilian Mügge (New York: Russell & Russell, 1964), pp. 113–114.

23. This is the thesis of Eugen Fink, the follower of Husserl, who held the legendary Heraclitus seminar with Martin Heidegger in the winter semester of 1966–1967; see Eugen Fink, *Nietzsche's Philosophy*, trans. Goetz Richter (New York: Continuum, 2003), p. 32; and for fragment B 52 Martin Heidegger, *The Principle of Reason*, trans. Reginald Lilly (Bloomington: Indiana University Press, 1991), pp. 112–113.

24. Nietzsche, "Philosophy During the Tragic Age of the Greeks," p. 108.

25. Jacob Bernays, "Heraklitische Studien," *Rheinisches Museum für Philologie* 7 (1849): pp. 90–116, here pp. 109–111.

26. Alexander Pope renders the passage as follows: "The hosts rush on; loud clamors shake the shore; / The horses thunder, earth and ocean roar! / Apollo, planted at the trench's bound, / Pushed at the bank: down sank the enormous mound: / Roll'd in the ditch the heapy ruin lay; / A sudden road! a long and ample way. / O'er the dread fosse (a late impervious space) / Now steeds, and men, and cars tumultuous pass. / The wondering crowds the downward level trod; / Before them flamed the shield, and march'd the god. / Then with his hand he shook the mighty wall; / And lo! the turrets nod, the bulwarks fall: / Easy as when ashore an infant stands, / And draws imagined houses in the sands; / The sportive wanton, pleased with some new play, / Sweeps the slights works and fashion'd domes away." Homer, *Iliad*, trans. Alexander Pope (North Charleston SC: Ex Fontibus, 2012), Book XV, p. 286.

27. See Günter Wohlfart, *Das spielende Kind. Nietzsche: Postvorsokratiker – Vorpostmoderner* (Essen: Die Blaue Eule, 1999), pp. 77–85.

28. Friedrich Nietzsche, *The Complete Works of Friedrich Nietzsche, vol. 15, The Will to Power*, ed. Oscar Levy, trans. Anthony M. Ludovici (New York: Russell & Russell, 1964), p. 430.

29. See for example Stephan K. Schindler, *Das Subjekt als Kind. Die Erfindung der Kindheit im Roman des 18. Jahrhunderts* (Berlin: Schmidt, 1994).

30. See Johan Huizinga, *Homo Ludens. Vom Ursprung der Kultur im Spiel* (Reinbeck bei Hamburg: Rowohlt, 1956).

31. See Jürgen Born, *Kafkas Bibliothek. Ein beschreibendes Verzeichnis* (Frankfurt am Main: Fischer, 1990), p. 119; and Patrick Bridgewater, *Kafka and Nietzsche* (Bonn: Bouvier, 1974), p. 10.

32. "Innocence is the child, and forgetfulness, a new beginning, a game, a self-rolling wheel rolling, a first movement, a holy Yea." Friedrich Nietzsche, *The Complete Works of Friedrich Nietzsche, vol. 11, Thus Spoke Zarathustra*, ed. Oscar Levy, trans. Thomas Common (New York: Russell & Russell, 1964), p. 27.

33. Referring to Lewis Carroll's *Alice in Wonderland* as part of his Plato interpretation, Gilles Deleuze will speak of an "ideal game." See Gilles Deleuze, *Logic of Sense*, trans. Mark Lester and Charles Stivale (New York: Columbia University Press, 1990). Strangely without naming Heraclitus, Deleuze sees Aion at work—fully Nietzschean— where the game, as in dice, "make[s] chance into an object of affirmation" (p. 60). His interpretation of the relationship between "Aion" and "Chronos" is also to be read in this way: while *Chronos* refers to the physical time of the body based on the model of the cyclical motions of the celestial spheres, Deleuze defines the unmoving aeon of eternity and ideational time as "empty form" (p. 62) and "empty present" (p. 63).

34. See Benjamin, *Selected Writings*, vol. 2, p. 799, where he quotes Kafka, *The Complete Stories*, p. 368.

35. Ibid., pp. 368–369.

36. Ibid., p. 369.

37. See Marianne Schuller and Gunnar Schmidt, *Mikrologien. Literarische und philosophische Figuren des Kleinen* (Bielefeld: transcript, 2003), pp. 100–112.

38. Kafka, The *Complete Stories*, p. 369.

39. Ibid., p. 362.

40. Ibid., p. 367.

41. Ibid., p. 370.

42. Ibid., pp. 427–429.

43. Ibid., p. 444.

44. Kafka, *Abandoned Fragments*, p. 203.

45. Kafka, *The Blue Octavo Notebooks*, p. 57.

46. Kafka, *Abandoned Fragments*, p. 142.

47. Ibid., p. 180.

48. Ibid., p. 224.

49. See Agamben, "In Playland. Reflections on History and Play," *Infancy and History*, pp. 75–96.

50. Claude Lévi-Strauss, *The Savage Mind*, trans. Doreen and John Weightman (Chicago: The University of Chicago Press, 1966), pp. 31–32.

51. "He knocked at the pillared door, while taking his top hat into his black-gloved right hand. The door was opened at once; It was opened immediately, and about fifty little boys lined both sides of the long hallway and bowed. The boatman came down the steps, greeted the gentleman, led him upstairs, on the second floor he walked with him around the court enclosed by slight loggias and, with the boys crowding after them at a respectful distance, the two men entered a cool, large room at the back of the house [...]." Kafka, *Abandoned Fragments*, p. 165.

52. "Everything went according to plan. I tracked, fell, bled to death in a gorge, I was dead, and this bark was supposed to carry me to the afterworld." Ibid., p. 168.

53. Kafka, *The Blue Octavo Notebooks*, p. 16.

54. Chronological time is not simply suspended and brought to a stand-still in play, but modified and slowed. See Kafka's entry in the Octavo Notebook H: "But eternity is not temporality at a standstill." Ibid., p. 46.

## An Angel's Grace, a Devil's Grin

1. See Nikola Roßbach, *"Jedes Kind ein Christkind, jedes Kind ein Mörder." Kind- und Kindheitsmotivik im Werk von Marie-Luise Kaschnitz* (Tübingen and Basel: Francke, 1999).

2. Quoted from Ulrich Ott, ed., *Vom Schreiben I. Das weiße Blatt oder Wie anfangen?* (Marbach: Deutsche Schillergesellschaft, 1994), p. 32.

3. Ariès, *Centuries of Childhood*, pp. 98–124.

4. Ibid., p. 119

5. Ibid., pp. 109 and 111.

6. Koschorke, *The Holy Family*, p. 117.

7. Ibid., p. 118.

8. Ibid., p. 129.

9. Ibid., p. 128.

10. Ibid., p. 126.

11. Ibid., p. 130.

12. For the medical subtext of Schiller's treatise, see Cornelia Zumbusch, *Die Immunität der Klassik* (Frankfurt am Main: Suhrkamp, 2011), pp. 147–159.

13. Schiller, *Naïve and Sentimental Poetry*, p. 85.

14. See Alefeld, *Göttliche Kinder*, p. 51.

15. Schiller, *Naïve and Sentimental Poetry*, pp. 86–87 (emphasis in original).

16. Ibid., p. 85 (emphasis in original).

17. See Aleida Assmann, "Werden was wir waren. Anmerkungen zur Geschichte der Kindheitsidee," *Antike und Abendland* XXIV (1978): pp. 98–124, here p. 99.

18. Schiller, *Naïve and Sentimental Poetry*, p. 103.

19. Novalis, *Henry of Ofterdingen: A Romance*, trans. Frederik Stallknecht (Cambridge: John Owen, 1842), p. 209.

20. Schiller, *Naïve and Sentimental Poetry*, p. 90. (emphasis in original).

21. With reference to Fröbel's pedagogics, see Baader, *Die romantische Idee*, pp. 221–255; with reference to the "sense of mission" of Protestant education in the service of the modern state, see Koschorke, *The Holy Family*, pp. 129–133.

22. Ibid., p. 65.

23. Jacobus de Voragine, *The Golden Legend: Readings on the Saints*, trans. William Granger Ryan (Princeton: Princeton University Press, 2012), p. 167.

24. For an oedipal reading of the New Testament passion as reflected in the mirror story of Judas, which figures as a culturally threatening moment in the narration of the Holy Family, see Koschorke, *The Holy Family*, pp. 63–65.

25. For the basic Christian model underpinning modern educational doctrines, see the study by the religious studies scholar Edmund Hermsen, *Faktor Religion. Geschichte der Kindheit vom Mittelalter bis zur Gegenwart* (Cologne: Böhlau, 2006), pp. 114–137.

26. See Dieter Richter, "Hexen, kleine Teufel, Schwererziehbare. Zur Kulturgeschichte des 'bösen Kindes'," in *Was für Kinder. Aufwachsen in Deutschland. Ein Handbuch*, ed. Deutsches Jugendinstitut (Munich: Kösel, 1993), pp. 195–202, esp. pp. 195–198.

27. Christian Gotthilf Salzmann, *Konrad Kiefer oder Anweisung zu einer vernünftigen Erziehung der Kinder. Ein Buch für's Volk* [1796], ed. Theo Dietrich (Bad Heilbrunn: Klinkhardt, 1961), p. 37.

28. See Rutschky, *Schwarze Pädagogik*.

29. See Kuhn, *Corruption in Paradise*; Sabine Büssing, *Aliens in the Home. The Child in Horror Fiction* (New York: Greenwood Press, 1987); Gertrud Lehnert, "Kindheit als Alterität. Zur Dämonisierung von Kindern in der Literatur der Moderne," in *Bücher haben ihre Geschichte: Kinder- und Jugendliteratur, Literatur und Nationalsozialismus, Deutschdidaktik*, ed. Petra Josting and Jan Wirrer (Hildesheim: Olms, 1996), pp. 246–261; Karen J. Renner, ed., *The 'Evil Child' in Literature, Film, and Popular Culture* (New York: Routledge, 2013); Nina Schimmel, *Grausame Unschuld. Zur Ambivalenz des bösen Kindes im Horrorfilm* (Berlin: Lit., 2015); Nicola Gess, "Böse Kinder. Zu einer literarischen und psychologischen Figur um 1900 (Lombroso, Wulffen), 1950 (Golding, March) und 2000 (Hustvedt, Shriver)," in Giuriato, *Kindheit und Literatur*, pp. 285–307.

30. See Hermsen, *Faktor Religion*, p. 161.

31. Hans Malmede, "Vom 'Genius des Bösen' oder: Die 'Entartung' von Minderjährigen. Negative Kindheitsbilder und defensive Modernisierung in der Epoche des Deutschen Kaiserreichs 1871–1918," in *Kinderwelten*, ed. Christa Berg (Frankfurt am Main: Suhrkamp, 1991), pp. 187–214.

32. Lombroso, *Criminal Man*, p. 190.

33. See for example Erich Wulffen, *Das Kind. Sein Wesen und seine Entartung* (Berlin: Langenscheidt, 1913), pp. 139–147.

34. See Gess, *Primitives Denken*, pp. 77–84, esp. p. 79.

35. Gustav Siegert, *Problematische Kindesnaturen. Eine Studie für Schule und Haus* (Kreuznach and Leipzig: Voigtländer, 1889), pp. 11–12.

36. Ibid., p. 13.

37. See Freud, *Standard Edition*, vol. VII, pp. 192–193: "Cruelty in general comes easily to the childish nature, since the obstacle that brings the instinct for mastery to a halt at another person's pain—namely a capacity for pity—is developed relatively late."

38. See Stephen Kern, "Freud und die Entdeckung der kindlichen Sexualität," *Kindheit. Zeitschrift zur Erforschung der psychischen Entwicklung* 1 (1979): pp. 215–238.

39. Koschorke, *The Holy Family*, p. 171.

40. Kafka, *The Complete Stories*, p. 87.

# Acknowledgements

## Texts

*Introduction*—written for the present volume, 2020.

*Idylls of Childhood*—written in February 2016 for a conference at the University of Zurich; first published in *Prekäre Idyllen in der Erzählliteratur des deutschsprachigen Realismus*, edited by Sabine Schneider and Marie Drath, pp. 118–131. Stuttgart: J. B. Metzler, 2017. Revised.

*Christmas*—written in February 2019; first published in *Fest/Schrift. Festschrift für Barbara Naumann*, edited by Georges Felten, Sophie Witt et al., pp. 153–157. Bielefeld: transcript, 2019. Revised.

*Rescuing Children*—based on lectures at the following universities: Vienna, Essen, and Princeton, held in 2012, 2013, and 2014, respectively; first published in *Internationales Archiv für Sozialgeschichte der deutschen Literatur* 40, no. 2 (2015): pp. 441–458. Revised.

*On the Threshold of Writing*—an earlier and very different version was published in *Poetica. Zeitschrift für Sprach- und Literaturwissenschaft* 42, no. 3–4 (2010): pp. 225–251.

*Becoming–Child*—an earlier and very different version was published in *Ferne Nähe. Neue Beiträge zu Robert Walser*, edited by Wolfram Groddeck, Reto Sorg and Peter Utz, pp. 125–132. Munich: Fink, 2007.

*Little Hans*—based on lectures at the Ludwig Maximilians University Munich and the Technische University Dortmund, in 2011 and 2012, respectively; first published in *Was der Fall ist. Casus und Lapsus*, edited by Inka Mülder-Bach and Michael Ott, pp. 129–143. Munich: Fink, 2015. Revised.

*This Briefest Childhood*—written in February 2008 for a conference at the University of Zurich; first published in *Schrift und Zeit in Franz Kafkas Oktavheften*, edited by Caspar Battegay, Felix Christen, and Wolfram Groddeck, pp. 101–117. Göttingen: Wallstein, 2010. Revised.

*An Angel's Grace, a Devil's Grin*—based on a guest lecture given at the Freie University Berlin in 2018; written for the present volume in 2020.

# Figures

1–4 Heinrich Hoffmann: *Lustige Geschichten und drollige Bilder, mit 20 schön colorirten Tafeln, für Kinder von 3 – 6 Jahren*, Frankfurt am Main, 1846, pp. 5–8.

5 Walter Benjamin: *A writing child* (1929). © Akademie der Künste / Academy of Arts (Berlin), Walter Benjamin Archive, Ms 733

6 Robert Walser, *Microscript Sheet 480r* (1925). © Keystone / Robert Walser-Foundation (Bern)

7 M. Klempfner, *Franz Kafka* (Prague, 1888). © Getty Images / ullstein bild Deutschland

8 Henri Cartier-Bresson, *Moment in Time* (Palermo, Italy, 1971). © Keystone / MAGNUM PHOTOS / Henri Cartier-Bresson

9 Rembrandt Harmensz. van Rijn, *Holy Family* (1645), Oil on canvas, 117 x 91 cm, St. Petersburg (Russia): The Hermitage Museum. Photograph © The State Hermitage Museum / photo by Vladimir Terebenin

***

I would like to warmly thank David Pister (Harvard University) for the careful and thoughtful editing and proof-reading of this volume.

# Bibliography

Agamben, Giorgio. *Infancy and History*. Translated by Liz Heron. London: Verso, 2007.

Agamben, Giorgio. *Profanations*. Translated by Jeff Fort. New York: Zone Books, 2007.

Agamben, Giorgio. *The Idea of Prose*. Translated by Michael Sullivan and Sam Whitsitt. Albany: State University of New York Press, 1995.

Agamben, Giorgio. *The Time That Remains. A Commentary on the Letter to the Romans*. Translated by Patricia Dailey. Stanford: Stanford University Press, 2005.

Aichele, Alexander. *Philosophie als Spiel. Platon – Kant – Nietzsche*. Berlin: De Gruyter, 2000.

Alefeld, Yvonne-Patricia. *Göttliche Kinder. Die Kindheitsideologie in der Romantik*. Paderborn: Schöningh, 1996.

Alt, Peter-André. *Franz Kafka. Der ewige Sohn*. Munich: C.H. Beck, 2005.

Anz, Thomas. "Psychoanalyse." In *Kafka-Handbuch. Leben – Werk – Wirkung*, edited by Bernd Auerochs and Manfred Engel, pp. 65–72. Stuttgart: Metzler, 2010.

Ariès, Philippe. *Centuries of Childhood: A Social History of Family Life*. Translated by Robert Baldick. London: Pimlico, 1996.

Assmann, Aleida. "Werden was wir waren. Anmerkungen zur Geschichte der Kindheitsidee." *Antike und Abendland* XXIV (1978): pp. 98–124.

Baader, Meike Sophia. *Die romantische Idee des Kindes und der Kindheit. Auf der Suche nach der verlorenen Unschuld*. Berlin: Luchterhand, 1996.

Baader, Meike Sophia, Florian Eßer, and Wolfgang Schröer, eds. *Kindheiten in der Moderne. Eine Geschichte der Sorge*. Frankfurt am Main and New York: Campus Verlag, 2014.

Begemann, Christian. *Die Welt der Zeichen. Stifter-Lektüren*. Stuttgart: Metzler, 1995.

Begemann, Christian and Davide Giuriato, eds. *Stifter-Handbuch. Leben – Werk – Wirkung*. Stuttgart: Metzler, 2017.

Benjamin, Walter. *Gesammelte Schriften*, edited by Rolf Tiedemann and Herrmann Schweppenhäuser. 7 Volumes. Frankfurt am Main: Suhrkamp, 1989.

Benjamin, Walter. *Selected Writings*, edited by Michael W. Jennings, Howard Eiland, Gary Smith. 4 Volumes. Translated by Rodney Livingstone and others. Cambridge MA and London: Harvard University Press, 2005.

Benjamin, Walter. *The Correspondence of Walter Benjamin, 1910–1940*. Translated by Manfred and Evelyn Jacobson. Chicago: University of Chicago Press, 1994.

Bernays, Jacob. "Heraklitische Studien." *Rheinisches Museum für Philologie* 7 (1849): pp. 90–116.

Bernert, Günther and Hans Hattenhauer, eds. *Allgemeines Landrecht für die Preußischen Staaten von 1794*. Neuwied: Luchterhand, 1994.

Binder, Hartmut. "Der Jäger Gracchus. Zu Kafkas Schaffensweise und poetischer Topographie." *Jahrbuch der deutschen Schillergesellschaft* 15 (1971): pp. 375–440.

Binder, Hartmut. *Kafka: Der Schaffensprozeß*. Frankfurt am Main: Suhrkamp, 1983.

Blasius, Dirk. *Ehescheidung in Deutschland im 19. und 20. Jahrhundert*. Frankfurt am Main: Fischer, 1992.

Boardman Smuts, Alice. *Science in the Service of Children, 1893–1935*. New Haven and London: Yale University Press, 2008.

Boas, George. *The Cult of Childhood*. London: Warburg Institute, 1966.

Bokma, Horst. *Das pädagogische Experiment des Schreibenden. Untersuchungen zu Walter Benjamins Rezensionen pädagogischer Literatur von 1924 bis 1932*. Frankfurt am Main: Lang, 2000.

Born, Jürgen. *Kafkas Bibliothek. Ein beschreibendes Verzeichnis*. Frankfurt am Main: Fischer, 1990.

Böschenstein, Renate. "Idyllisch/Idylle." In *Ästhetische Grundbegriffe*, edited by Karlheinz Barck, Martin Fontius, and Dieter Schlenstedt, volume 3, pp. 119–137. Stuttgart: Metzler, 2010.

Bridgewater, Patrick. *Kafka and Nietzsche*. Bonn: Bouvier, 1974.

Brüggemann, Heinz. *Walter Benjamin. Über Spiel, Farbe und Phantasie*. Würzburg: Königshausen & Neumann, 2011.

Buck-Morss, Susan. *The Dialectics of Seeing: Walter Benjamin and the Arcades Project*. Cambridge MA: MIT Press, 1989.

Bühler, Karl. *Die geistige Entwicklung des Kindes*. Jena: Fischer, 1918.

Bühler, Karl. *The Mental Development of the Child, a Summary of Modern Psychological Theory*. Translated by Oscar Oeser. New York: Harcourt, Brace & Co., 1930.

Büssing, Sabine. *Aliens in the Home. The Child in Horror Fiction*. New York: Greenwood Press, 1987.

Clarke Hall, William. *The State and the Child*. London: Friedrich A. Stokes Company, 1917.

Classen, Albrecht, ed. *Childhood in the Middle Ages and Renaissance*. Berlin and New York: Walter de Gruyter, 2005.

Cunningham, Hugh. *Children and Childhood in Western Society Since 1500*. London and New York: Routledge, 2005.

Cunningham, Hugh. *The Invention of Childhood*. London: BBC Books, 2006.

Deckert-Peaceman, Heike, Cornelie Dietrich, and Ursula Stenger, eds. *Einführung in die Kindheitsforschung*. Darmstadt: WBG, 2010.

Degani, Enzo. *Aion*. Bologna: Pàtron, 1957.

Deleuze, Gilles. *Logic of Sense*. Translated by Mark Lester and Charles Stivale. New York: Columbia University Press, 1990.

Depaepe, Marc. *Zum Wohl des Kindes? Pädologie, pädagogische Psychologie und experimentelle Pädagogik in Europa und den USA, 1890–1940*. Weinheim: Deutscher Studien Verlag, 1993.

Doderer, Klaus, ed. *Walter Benjamin und die Kinderliteratur. Aspekte der Kinderkultur in den zwanziger Jahren*. Weinheim and Munich: Juventa, 1988.

Douthwaite, Julia. "Rewriting the Savage: The Extraordinary Fictions of the Wild Girl of Champagne." *Eighteenth Century Studies* 28, no. 2 (1994/95): pp. 163–192.

Enzinger, Moriz. *Adalbert Stifter im Urteil seiner Zeit*. Vienna: Böhlau, 1968.

Ewers, Hans-Heino, *Kindheit als poetische Daseinsform. Studien zur Entstehung der romantischen Kindheitsutopie im 18. Jahrhundert. Herder, Jean Paul, Novalis, Tieck*. Munich: Fink, 1989.

Fink, Eugen. *Nietzsche's Philosophy*. Translated by Goetz Richter. New York: Continuum, 2003.

Foucault, Michel. *Discipline and Punish. The Birth of the Prison*. Translated by Alan Sheridan. London: Penguin, 1985.

Foucault, Michel. *The History of Sexuality. Volume I: An Introduction*. Translated by Robert Hurley. London: Penguin, 1981.

Foucault, Michel. *Mental Illness and Psychology*. Translated by Alan Sheridan. Berkley: University of California Press, 1997.

Franz, Marie-Louise von, *Der ewige Jüngling. Der Puer aeternus und der kreative Genius im Erwachsenen*. Munich: Kösel, 1987.

Freud, Sigmund. *The Standard Edition of the Complete Psychological Works of Sigmund Freud*. Translated by James Strachey. 24 Volumes. London: Vintage, 2001.

Fröbel, Friedrich. "Entwurf eines Planes zur Begründung und Ausführung eines KINDER-GARTENS [1840]." In Friedrich Fröbel. *Ausgewählte Schriften*, edited by Erika Hoffmann, vol. 1 Kleine Schriften und Briefe von 1809–1851, pp. 114–125. Godesberg: Küpper, 1951.

Gamper, Michael. "Wetterrätsel. Zu Adalbert Stifters *Kazensilber*." In *Literatur und Nicht-Wissen. Historische Konstellationen 1730–1930*, edited by Michael Bies and Michael Gamper, pp. 325–338. Zurich: Diaphanes, 2012.

Geisenhanslüke, Achim. "Kafkas schmutzige Kinder. Schwellenerfahrungen in *Der Verschollene*." In *Liminale Anthropologien. Zwischenzeiten, Schwellenphänomene, Zwischenräume in Literatur und Philosophie*, edited by Jochen Achilles, Roland Borgards, and Brigitte Burrichter, pp. 199–208. Würzburg: Königshausen & Neumann, 2012.

Geulen, Eva. "Adalbert Stifters Kinder-Kunst. Drei Fallstudien." *Deutsche Vierteljahresschrift für Literaturwissenschaft und Geistesgeschichte* 67 (1993): pp. 648–668.

Geulen, Eva. "Erziehungsakte." In *Rhetorik: Figuration und Performanz*, edited by Jürgen Fohrmann, pp. 629–652. Stuttgart and Weimar: Metzler, 2004.

Geulen, Eva. "Kinderlos." *Internationales Archiv für Sozialgeschichte der deutschen Literatur* 40, no. 2 (2015): pp. 420–440.

Geulen, Eva. "Legislating Education. Kant, Hegel, and Benjamin on Pedagogical Violence." *Cardozo Law Review* 26, no. 3 (2005): pp. 943–956.

Geulen, Eva. *Worthörig wider Willen. Darstellungsproblematik und Sprachreflexion in der Prosa Adalbert Stifters*. Munich: ludicium, 1992.

Gess, Nicola. "Böse Kinder. Zu einer literarischen und psychologischen Figur um 1900 (Lombroso, Wulffen), 1950 (Golding, March) und 2000 (Hustvedt, Shriver)." In *Kindheit und Literatur. Konzepte – Poetik – Wissen*, edited by Davide Giuriato, Philipp Hubmann, and Mareike Schildmann, pp. 285–307. Freiburg im Breisgau: Rombach, 2018.

Gess, Nicola. *Primitives Denken. Wilde Kinder und Wahnsinnige in der literarischen Moderne (Müller, Musil, Benn, Benjamin)*. Munich: Fink, 2013.

Gisi, Lucas Marco. *Robert Walser Handbuch. Leben – Werk – Wirkung*. Stuttgart: Metzler, 2015.

Giuriato, Davide, Philipp Hubmann, and Mareike Schildmann, eds. *Kindheit und Literatur. Konzepte – Poetik – Wissen*. Freiburg im Breisgau: Rombach, 2018.

Giuriato, Davide. *Mikrographien. Zu einer Poetologie des Schreibens in Walter Benjamins Kindheitserinnerungen (1932–1939)*. Munich: Fink, 2006.

Giuriato, Davide. "'Wolf der Wüste.' Michael Kohlhaas und die Rettung des Lebens." In *Ausnahmezustand der Literatur. Neue Lektüren zu Heinrich von Kleist*, edited by Nicolas Pethes, pp. 290–306. Göttingen: Wallstein, 2011.

Goethe, Johann Wolfgang. *Wilhelm Meister's Apprenticeship*. Translated by Eric A. Blackall. Princeton: Princeton University Press, 1995.

Gontard, Alexander von. "The Development of Child Psychiatry in Nineteenth Century Britain." *Journal of Child Psychology and Psychiatry* 29 (1988): pp. 569–588.

Grimm, Jacob and Wilhelm. *Deutsches Wörterbuch*. 33 Volumes. Leipzig: Hirzel, 1854–1960.

Gstettner, Peter. *Die Eroberung des Kindes durch die Wissenschaft. Aus der Geschichte der Disziplinierung*. Reinbek bei Hamburg: Rowohlt, 1981.

Haefcke, Hermann. *Handbuch des Abdeckereiwesens* [1906]. Oldenburg: Olms, 2006.

Heidegger, Martin. *The Principle of Reason*. Translated by Reginald Lilly. Bloomington: Indiana University Press, 1991.

Herder, Johann Gottfried. "The Idyll." In *The Ladies' Magazine*, edited by Sarah Hale. Translated by J. N. Nichols, pp. 422–423. Boston: Putnam & Hunt, 1829.

Hermann, Ruth. *Im Zwischenraum zwischen Welt und Spielzeug. Eine Poetik der Kindheit bei Rilke*. Würzburg: Königshausen & Neumann, 2002.

Hermsen, Edmund. *Faktor Religion. Geschichte der Kindheit vom Mittelalter bis zur Gegenwart*. Cologne: Böhlau, 2006.

Hertling, Gunter H. "Mignons Schwestern im Erzählwerk Adalbert Stifters *Katzensilber, Der Waldbrunnen, Die Narrenburg*." In *Goethes Mignon und ihre Schwestern. Interpretationen und Rezeption,* edited by Gerhart Hoffmeister, pp. 165–197. New York: Lang, 1993.

Hinz, Klaus-Michael. "Wo die bösen Kinder wohnen. Robert Walsers Melancholie. Mit einer Fußnoten zu Kafkas Spielsachen." In *Robert Walser*, edited by Klaus-Michael Hinz and Thomas Horst, pp. 310–322. Frankfurt am Main: Suhrkamp, 1991.

Hoffmann, Christoph. *Unter Beobachtung. Naturforschung in der Zeit der Sinnesapparate*. Göttingen: Wallstein, 2006.

Hoffmann, E.T.A. *The Strange Child*. Translated by Anthea Bell. London: Pushkin Press, 2010.

Hoffman, Heinrich. *Slovenly Peter, or: Cheerful Stories and Funny Pictures for Good Little Folks*. Translated by Mark Twain. Philadelphia: Porter and Coates, 1931.

Homer. *Iliad*. Translated by Alexander Pope. North Charleston SC: Ex Fontibus, 2012.

Huizinga, Johan. *Homo Ludens. Vom Ursprung der Kultur im Spiel*. Reinbeck bei Hamburg: Rowohlt, 1956.

Jean Paul. *Horn of Oberon. Jean Paul Richter's School for Aesthetics*. Translated by Margaret Hale. Detroit: Wayne State University Press, 1973.

Jenks, Chris. *Childhood*. London and New York: Routledge, 1996.

Jens, Walter, ed. *Es begibt sich aber zu der Zeit. Texte zur Weihnachtsgeschichte*. Frankfurt am Main: Fischer Klassik, 2012.

Kafka, Franz. *Abandoned Fragments. Unedited Works 1897–1917*. Translated by Ina Pfitzner. New York: Sun Vision Books, 2012.

Kafka, Franz. *Beim Bau der Chinesischen Mauer*. Munich: Gustav Kiepenheuer, 1931.

Kafka, Franz. *Historisch-kritische Ausgabe sämtlicher Handschriften, Drucke und Typoskripte. Oxforder Oktavheft 1 & 2*, edited by Roland Reuß and Peter Staengle. Frankfurt am Main and Basel: Stroemfeld, 2006.

Kafka, Franz. *The Blue Octavo Notebooks*, edited by Max Brod. Translated by Ernst Kaiser and Eithne Wilkins. New York: Schocken Books, 1954.

Kafka, Franz. *The Castle*. Translated by Mark Harman. New York: Schocken Books, 1998.

Kafka, Franz. *The Complete Stories*. Translated by Willa and Edwin Muir. New York: Schocken Books, 1971.

Kafka, Franz. *The Diaries of Franz Kafka 1910–1913*, edited Max Brod. Translated by Joseph Kresh. New York: Schocken Books, 1948.

Kafka, Franz. *The Diaries of Franz Kafka 1914–1922*, edited by Max Brod. Translated by Martin Greenberg. New York: Schocken Books, 1949.

Kammer, Stephan. *Figurationen und Gesten des Schreibens. Zur Ästhetik der Produktion in Robert Walsers Prosa der Berner Zeit*. Tübingen: Max Niemeyer Verlag, 2003.

Kaufmann, Franz-Xaver. "Kinder als Außenseiter der Gesellschaft." *Merkur. Zeitschrift für europäisches Denken* 34, no. 8 (1980): pp. 761–771.

Kern, Stephen. "Freud und die Entdeckung der kindlichen Sexualität." *Kindheit. Zeitschrift zur Erforschung der psychischen Entwicklung* 1 (1979): pp. 215–238.

Key, Ellen. *The Century of the Child*. New York, London: G. P. Putnam's and Sons, 1909.

Kinzel, Ulrich. *Ethische Projekte. Literatur und Selbstgestaltung im Kontext des Regierungsdenkens. Humboldt, Goethe, Stifter, Raabe*. Frankfurt am Main: Klostermann, 2000.

Kittler, Friedrich A. *Discourse Networks 1800/1900*. Translated by Michael Metteer and Chris Cullens. Stanford: Stanford University Press, 1990.

Klein, Reimar. *"Sieh einmal, hier steht er!" Struwwelpeters beschädigte Kinderwelt*. Frankfurt am Main: Insel, 2005.

Kleinwort, Malte. *Der späte Kafka – Spätstil als Stilsuspension.* Munich: Fink, 2013.

Könneker, Marie-Luise. *Dr. Heinrich Hoffmanns 'Struwwelpeter.' Untersuchungen zur Entstehungs- und Funktionsgeschichte eines bürgerlichen Bilderbuches.* Stuttgart: Metzler, 1977.

Koschorke, Albrecht. "Das buchstabierte Panorama: Zu einer Passage in Stifters Erzählung *Granit.*" *Vierteljahresschrift des Adalbert Stifter-Instituts* 38 (1989): pp. 3–13.

Koschorke, Albrecht. "Erziehung zum Freitod. Adalbert Stifters pädagogischer Realismus." In *Die Dinge und die Zeichen. Dimensionen des Realistischen in der Erzählliteratur des 19. Jahrhunderts,* edited by Sabine Schneider and Barbara Hunfeld, pp. 319–332. Würzburg: Königshausen & Neumann, 2008.

Koschorke, Albrecht. "Kindermärchen. Liminalität in der Biedermeierfamilie." In Albrecht Koschorke, Nacim Ghanbari, Eva Eßlinger, Sebastian Susteck, Michael Thomas Taylor. *Vor der Familie. Grenzbedingungen einer modernen Institution,* pp. 139–171. Munich: Konstanz University Press, 2010.

Koschorke, Albrecht. *The Holy Family and its Legacy. Religious Imagination from the Gospels to Star Wars.* Translated by Thomas Dunlap. New York: Columbia University Press, 2003.

Krause, Marcus. "'Seelensucher'. Freuds *Bruchstück einer Hysterie-Analyse* als Versuchsanordnung zwischen Literatur und Wissenschaft." In *"Es ist ein Laboratorium, ein Laboratorium für Worte." Experiment und Literatur III, 1890–2010,* edited by Michael Bies and Michael Gamper, pp. 72–95. Göttingen: Wallstein, 2011.

Kremer, Detlef. "Idyll und Trauma. Kindheit in der Romantik." *E.T.A. Hoffmann Jahrbuch* 11 (2003): pp. 7–18.

Küenzlen, Gottfried. *Der Neue Mensch. Eine Untersuchung zur säkularen Religionsgeschichte der Moderne.* Frankfurt am Main: Suhrkamp, 1997.

Kugler, Stefani. "Katastrophale Ordnung. Natur und Kultur in Adalbert Stifters Erzählung Kazensilber." In *Poetische Ordnungen. Zur Erzählprosa des deutschen Realismus,* edited by Ulrich Kittstein and Stefani Kugler, pp. 121–141. Würzburg: Königshausen & Neumann, 2007.

Kuhn, Reinhard. *Corruption in Paradise. The Child in Western Literature.* Hanover NH and London: University of New England Press, 1982.

Lacan, Jacques. *La relation d'objet. Le Seminaire. Livre IV.* Paris: Seuil, 1998.

Lackeit, Conrad. *Aion. Zeit und Ewigkeit in Sprache und Religion der Griechen.* Königsberg: Hartungsche Buchdruckerei, 1916.

Lane, Harlan. *The Wild Boy of Aveyron.* Cambridge MA: Harvard University Press, 1976.

Lehmann, Johannes and Hubert Thüring, eds. *Rettung und Erlösung. Politisches Heil in der Moderne.* Munich: Fink, 2015.

Lehnert, Gertrud. "Kindheit als Alterität. Zur Dämonisierung von Kindern in der Literatur der Moderne." In *Bücher haben ihre Geschichte: Kinder- und Jugendliteratur, Literatur und Nationalsozialismus, Deutschdidaktik*, edited by Petra Josting and Jan Wirrer, pp. 246–261. Hildesheim: Olms, 1996.

Lenzen, Dieter. "Kulturgeschichte der Vaterschaft." In *Wann ist der Mann ein Mann? Zur Geschichte der Männlichkeit*, edited by Walter Erhart and Britta Herrmann, pp. 87–113. Stuttgart and Weimar: Metzler, 1997.

Leslie, Esther. "Colonial and Capitalist Pedagogy." *Pedagogy, Culture & Society* 24, no. 4 (2016): pp. 517–524.

Lévi-Strauss, Claude. *The Savage Mind.* Translated by Doreen and John Weightman. Chicago: The University of Chicago Press, 1966.

Lindner, Burkhardt, ed. *Benjamin-Handbuch. Leben – Werk – Wirkung.* Stuttgart: Metzler, 2011.

Lloyd, Rosemary. *The Land of Lost Content. Children and Childhood in Nineteenth-Century French Literature.* Oxford: Clarendon, 1992.

Lombroso, Cesare. *Criminal Man.* Translated by Mary Gibson and Nicole Hahn Rafter. Durham NC and London: Duke University Press, 2006.

Ludwig, Otto. *Der Schulaufsatz. Seine Geschichte in Deutschland.* Berlin: De Gruyter, 1988.

Lüdemann, Susanne. "Literarische Fallgeschichten. Schillers *Verbrecher aus verlorener Ehre* und Kleists *Michael Kohlhaas*." In *Das Beispiel. Epistemologie des Exemplarischen*, edited by Jens Ruchatz, Stefan Willer, and Nicolas Pethes, pp. 208–223. Berlin: Kadmos, 2007.

Lüdemann, Susanne. *Mythos und Selbstdarstellung. Zur Poetik der Psychoanalyse.* Freiburg im Breisgau: Rombach, 1994.

Luhmann, Niklas. "Das Kind als Medium der Erziehung." In Niklas Luhmann, *Schriften zur Pädagogik*, edited by Dieter Lenzen, pp. 159–186. Frankfurt am Main: Suhrkamp, 2004.

Lyotard, Jean-François. *Lectures d'enfance.* Paris: Éditions Galilée, 1991.

Mall-Grob, Beatrice. *Fiktion des Anfangs. Literarische Kindheitsmodelle bei Jean Paul und Adalbert Stifter.* Stuttgart and Weimar: Metzler, 1999.

Malmede, Hans. "Vom 'Genius des Bösen' oder: Die 'Entartung' von Minderjährigen. Negative Kindheitsbilder und defensive Modernisierung in der Epoche des Deutschen Kaiserreichs 1871–1918." In *Kinderwelten*, edited by Christa Berg, pp. 187–214. Frankfurt am Main: Suhrkamp, 1991.

Malson, Lucien, Jean Itard, Octave Mannoni. *Die wilden Kinder.* Frankfurt am Main: Suhrkamp, 1972.

Mattenklott, Gundel. "Phantastische Ländchen. Beiträge zu einem historisch-literarischen Atlas der Kindheit." In *Topographien der Kindheit. Literarische, mediale und interdisziplinäre Perspektiven auf Orts- und Raumkonstruktionen*, edited by Caroline Roeder, pp. 301–312. Bielefeld: transcript, 2013.

Mehlmann, Jeffrey. *Walter Benjamin for Children. An Essay on his Radio Years.* Chicago: University of Chicago Press, 1993.

Michaelis, Tatjana. *Der romantische Kindheitsmythos. Kindheitsdarstellungen der französischen Literatur von Rousseau bis zum Ende der Romantik.* Frankfurt am Main: Lang, 1986.

Middleton, Christopher. "A Parenthesis to the Discussion of Robert Walser's Schizophrenia." In *Robert Walser Rediscovered. Stories, fairy-tale plays, and critical responses*, edited by Mark Harman, pp. 190–194. Hanover NH and London: University Press of New England, 1985.

Morgenstern, Lina. *Das Paradies der Kindheit, Eine ausführliche Anleitung für Mütter und Erzieherinnen zur Kindespflege und Erziehung in den ersten sechs Jahren und zur praktischen Anwendung von Friedrich Fröbel's Spielbeschäftigungen in Haus und Kindergarten [1861].* Vienna: Bichler, 1889.

Morlang, Werner. "Melusines Hinterlassenschaft. Zur Demystifikation und Remystifikation von Robert Walsers Mikrographie." *Runa* 21 (1994): pp. 81–99.

Nägele, Rainer. "Auf der Suche nach dem verlorenen Paradies. Versuch einer Interpretation zu Kafkas *Der Jäger Gracchus*." *The German Quarterly* 47, no. 1 (1974): pp. 60–72.

Neumann, Gerhard. "Die Arbeit im Alchimistengäßchen (1916–1917)." In *Kafka-Handbuch,* edited by Hartmut Binder, vol. 2, pp. 313–350. Stuttgart: Kröner, 1979.

Neumann, Gerhard. "Franz Kafka: Der Name, die Sprache und die Ordnung der Dinge." In *Franz Kafka: Schriftverkehr*, edited by Wolf Kittler and Gerhard Neumann, pp. 11–29. Freiburg im Breisgau: Rombach, 1990.

Neumann, Gerhard. "Nachrichten vom Pontus. Das Problem der Kunst im Werk Franz Kafkas." In *Franz Kafka: Schriftverkehr*, edited by Wolf Kittler and Gerhard Neumann, pp. 164–198. Freiburg im Breisgau: Rombach, 1990.

Neumann, Gerhard. "Puppe und Automate. Inszenierte Kindheit in E.T.A. Hoffmanns Sozialisationsmärchen Nußknacker und Mausekönig." In *Jugend – ein romantisches Konzept?*, edited by Günter Oesterle, pp. 135–160. Würzburg: Königshausen & Neumann, 1997.

Neve, Michael and Trevor Turner. "History of Child and Adolescent Psychiatry." In *Child and Adolescent Psychiatry*, edited by Michael Rutter and Eric Taylor, pp. 382–395. Oxford: Wiley, 2002.

Niedermeier, Michael. "Nützlichkeit und Mysterien der Mutter Natur. Pädagogische Gärten der Philanthropen." In *Der imaginierte Garten,* edited by Günter Oesterle and Harald Tausch, pp. 157–197. Göttingen: Vandenhoeck & Ruprecht, 2001.

Niehaus, Michael. *Das Verhör. Geschichte – Theorie – Fiktion.* Munich: Fink, 2003.

Nietzsche, Friedrich. *The Complete Works of Friedrich Nietzsche.* Edited by Oscar Levy. 18 Volumes. New York: Russell & Russell, 1964.

Nix, Angelika. *Das Kind des Jahrhunderts im Jahrhundert des Kindes. Zur Entstehung der phantastischen Erzählung in der schwedischen Kinderliteratur.* Freiburg im Breisgau: Rombach, 2002.

Novalis. *Henry of Ofterdingen: A Romance*. Translated by Frederik Stallknecht. Cambridge: John Owen, 1842.

Novalis. *Philosophical Writings*. Translated by Margaret Mahony Stoljar. Albany: Southern University of New York Press, 1997.

Oertel Sjörgen, Christine. "Myths and Metaphors in Stifter's Katzensilber." *The Journal of English and Germanic Philology* 86 (1987): pp. 358–371.

Ott, Ulrich, ed. *Vom Schreiben I. Das weiße Blatt oder Wie anfangen?* Marbach: Deutsche Schillergesellschaft, 1994.

Pannenberg, Wolfhart. "Mythos und Dogma im Weihnachtsfest." In *Das Fest,* edited by Walter Haug and Rainer Warning, pp. 53–63. Munich: Fink, 1989.

Pethes, Nicolas, ed. *Ausnahmezustand der Literatur. Neue Lektüren zu Heinrich von Kleist*. Göttingen: Wallstein, 2011.

Pethes, Nicolas. "Die Arbeit am Mythos 'Kindheit' bei Walter Benjamin." In *Kindheit und Literatur. Konzepte – Poetik – Wissen*, edited by Davide Giuriato, Philipp Hubmann, and Mareike Schildmann, pp. 57–73. Freiburg im Breisgau: Rombach, 2018.

Pethes, Nicolas. *Literarische Fallgeschichten. Zur Poetik einer epistemischen Schreibweise*. Göttingen: Wallstein, 2016.

Pethes, Nicolas. "Vom Einzelfall zur Menschheit. Die Fallgeschichte als Medium der Wissenspopularisierung zwischen Recht, Medizin und Literatur." In *Popularisierung und Popularität*, edited by Gereon Blaseio, Hedwig Pompe, and Jens Ruchatz, pp. 63–92. Cologne: DuMont, 2005.

Pethes, Nicolas. *Zöglinge der Natur. Der literarische Menschenversuch des 18. Jahrhunderts*. Göttingen: Wallstein, 2007.

Postman, Neil. *The Disappearance of Childhood*. New York: Delacorte Press, 1982.

Prade, Juliane. *Sprachoffenheit. Mensch, Tier und Kind in der Autobiographie*. Würzburg: Königshausen & Neumann, 2013.

Preyer, William T. *The Mind of the Child. Observations Concerning the Mental Development of the Human Being in the First Years of Life*. Translated by H. W. Brown. New York: D. Appleton & Co., 1893.

Ratschow, Carl Heinz, Josef Scharbert, Zeev W. Falk, Bo Reicke, Henri Crouzel, Leendert Brink, Maurice E. Schild, et al. "Ehe/Eherecht/ Ehescheidung." In *Theologische Realenzyklopädie*, edited by Gerhard Krause and Gerhard Müller. Vol. 9, pp. 308–311. Berlin and New York: de Gruyter, 1982.

Rehm, Walter. "Stifters Erzählung *Der Waldgänger* als Dichtung der Reue." In Walter Rehm, *Begegnungen und Probleme. Studien zur deutschen Literaturgeschichte,* pp. 317–345. Bern: Francke, 1957.

Renner, Karen J., ed. The *'Evil Child' in Literature, Film, and Popular Culture.* New York: Routledge, 2013.

Richter, Dieter. *Das fremde Kind. Zur Entstehung der Kindheitsbilder des bürgerlichen Zeitalters.* Frankfurt am Main: Fischer, 1987.

Richter, Dieter. "Hexen, kleine Teufel, Schwererziehbare. Zur Kulturgeschichte des 'bösen Kindes'." In *Was für Kinder. Aufwachsen in Deutschland. Ein Handbuch*, edited by Deutsches Jugendinstitut, pp. 195–202. Munich: Kösel, 1993.

Riehl, Wilhelm Heinrich. *The Natural History of the German People*, vol. 3. Translated by David J. Diephouse. Lewiston, Queenston, Lampeter: Edwin Mellen Press, 1990.

Rietmann, Felix, Mareike Schildmann, Caroline Arni, Daniel Thomas Cook, Davide Giuriato, Novina Göhlsdorf, and Wangui Muigai. "Knowledge of Childhood. Materiality, text, and the history of science – and interdisciplinary roundtable discussion." *British Journal for the History of Science* 50 (2017): pp. 111–141.

Rilke, Rainer Maria. *Letters of Rainer Maria Rilke 1892–1910.* Translated by Jane B. Greene and M. D. Herter Norton. New York: W. W. Norton & Company, 1945.

Rilke, Rainer Maria Rilke. *Letters on Life: New Prose Translations.* Translated by Ulrich Baer. New York: The Modern Library, 2006.

Rilke, Rainer Maria. *Sämtliche Werke.* Published by Rilke-Archiv in cooperation with Ruth Sieber-Rilke and Ernst Zinn. 7 Volumes. Frankfurt am Main: Insel, 1965.

Rilke, Rainer Maria. *Selected Works I: Prose.* Translated by G. Craig Houston. London: The Hogarth Press, 1954.

Rilke, Rainer Maria. *The Notebooks of Malte Laurens Brigge: A Novel.* Translated by Stephen Mitchell. New York: Vintage International, 1990.

Rilke, Rainer Maria. *The Poetry of Rilke*. Translated by Edward Snow. New York: North Point Press, 2009.

Rilke, Rainer Maria and Ellen Key. *Briefwechsel*, edited by Theodore Fiedler. Frankfurt am Main: Suhrkamp, 1993.

Rose, Wolfgang, Petra Fuchs, and Thomas Beddies. *Diagnose "Psychopathie". Die urbane Moderne und das "schwierige Kind." Berlin 1918–1933*. Vienna: Böhlau, 2016.

Roßbach, Nikola. *"Jedes Kind ein Christkind, jedes Kind ein Mörder." Kind- und Kindheitsmotivik im Werk von Marie-Luise Kaschnitz*. Tübingen and Basel: Francke, 1999.

Rousseau, Jean-Jacques. *Emile, or On Education*. Translated by Barbara Foxley. New York: E.P. Dutton, 1911.

Rutschky, Katharina, ed. *Schwarze Pädagogik. Quellen zur Naturgeschichte der bürgerlichen Erziehung*. Frankfurt am Main: Ullstein, 1977.

Salzmann, Christian Gotthilf. *Konrad Kiefer oder Anweisung zu einer vernünftigen Erziehung der Kinder. Ein Buch für's Volk* [1796], edited by Theo Dietrich. Bad Heilbrunn: Klinkhardt, 1961.

Saussure, Ferdinand de. *Linguistik und Semiologie: Notizen aus dem Nachlaß. Texte, Briefe und Dokumente*. Frankfurt am Main: Suhrkamp, 2003.

Schäffle, Albert Eberhard Friedrich. *Bau und Leben des socialen Körpers: encyclopädischer Entwurf einer realen Anatomie, Physiologie und Psychologie der menschlichen Gesellschaft: mit besonderer Rücksicht auf die Volkswirthschaft als socialen Stoffwechsel*. 3 Volumes. Tübingen: Laupp, 1875–1878.

Schildmann, Mareike. *Poetik der Kindheit. Literatur und Wissen bei Robert Walser*. Göttingen: Wallstein, 2019.

Schiller, Friedrich. *Naïve and Sentimental Poetry, and On the Sublime: Two Essays*. Translated by Julius A. Elias. New York: Ungar Publishing, 1984.

Schiller, Friedrich. *On the Aesthetic Education of Man, in a Series of Letters*. Translated by Reginald Snell. London: Routledge, 1954.

Schimmel, Nina. *Grausame Unschuld. Zur Ambivalenz des bösen Kindes im Horrorfilm*. Berlin: Lit., 2015.

Schindler, Stephan K. *Das Subjekt als Kind. Die Erfindung der Kindheit im Roman des 18. Jahrhunderts*. Berlin: Schmidt, 1994.

Schleiermacher, Friedrich. *Christmas Eve Celebration. A Dialogue*. Translated by Terrence N. Tice. Eugene: Cascade Books, 2010.

Scholem, Gershom. *Walter Benjamin. The Story of a Friendship*. Translated by Harry Zohn. New York: New York Review of Books, 2003.

Schonig, Bruno. "Reformpädagogik." In *Handbuch der deutsche Reformpädagogik 1880–1933,* edited by Diethart Kerbs and Jürgen Reulecke, pp. 319–330. Wuppertal: Hammer, 1998.

Schünemann, Peter. "Kindheitsmuseum Walter Benjamin." *Neue Rundschau* 103, no. 3 (1992): pp. 128–139.

Schütterle, Annette. *Franz Kafkas Oktavhefte: Ein Schreibprozeß als 'System des Teilbaues.'* Freiburg im Breisgau: Rombach, 2002.

Schuller, Marianne and Gunnar Schmidt. *Mikrologien. Literarische und philosophische Figuren des Kleinen*. Bielefeld: transcript, 2003.

Schultz, James A. *The Knowledge of Childhood in the German Middle Ages, 1100–1350*. Philadelphia: University of Pennsylvania Press, 1995.

Schwerin, Kerstin von. *Minima Aesthetica. Die Kunst des Verschwindens*. Frankfurt am Main: Lang, 2001.

Shahar, Sulamith. *Childhood in the Middle Ages*. London: Routledge, 1990.

Shorter, Edward. *The Making of the Modern Family*. New York: Collins, 1975.

Shuttleworth, Sally. *The Mind of the Child. Child Development in Literature, Science and Medicine, 1840–1900*. Oxford: Oxford University Press, 2010.

Siegert, Gustav. *Problematische Kindesnaturen. Eine Studie für Schule und Haus*. Kreuznach and Leipzig: Voigtländer, 1889.

Simonis, Annette. *Kindheit in Romanen um 1800*. Bielefeld: Aisthesis, 1993.

Steedman, Carolyn. *Strange Dislocations. Childhood and the Idea of Human Interiority (1780–1930)*. London: Virago, 1995.

Stein, Lorenz von. *System der Staatswissenschaft*. Vol. 1. Stuttgart and Tübingen: Cotta, 1852.

Steinlein, Rüdiger. "Das fremde Kind – Maternalität, Kindlichkeit und Phantasie. Das Märchen als antipädagogischer Diskurs." In *Die domestizierte Phantasie. Studien zur Kinderliteratur, Kinderlektüre und Literaturpädagogik des 18. und frühen 19. Jahrhunderts*, edited by Rüdiger Steinlein, pp. 236–242. Heidelberg: Winter, 1987.

Stiemer, Hendrik. *Über scheinbar naive und dilettantische Dichtung. Text- und Kontextstudien zu Robert Walser.* Würzburg: Königshausen & Neumann, 2014.

Stifter, Adalbert. *Rock Crystal. A Christmas Tale.* Translated by Elizabeth Mayer and Marianne Moore. New York: Pantheon Books, 1965.

Stifter, Adalbert. *Tales of Old Vienna and other Prose.* Translated by Alexander Stillmark. Riverside CA: Ariadne Press, 2016.

Stifter, Adalbert. *Werke und Briefe. Historisch-kritische Gesamtausgabe.* Edited by Alfred Doppler and Wolfgang Frühwald, since 2001 by Alfred Doppler and Hartmut Laufhütte. 33 volumes. Stuttgart: Kohlhammer, 1978.

Stoessel, Marleen. *Aura. Das vergessene Menschliche. Zu Sprache und Erfahrung bei Walter Benjamin.* Munich: Hanser, 1983.

Strelis, Joachim. *Die verschwiegene Dichtung. Reden, Schweigen, Verstummen im Werk Robert Walsers.* Frankfurt am Main: Lang, 1991.

Thomä, Dieter. *Väter. Eine moderne Heldengeschichte.* Munich: Hanser, 2008.

Tismar, Jens. *Gestörte Idyllen. Über Jean Paul, Adalbert Stifter, Robert Walser und Thomas Bernhard.* Munich: Hanser, 1973.

Turmel, André. *A Historical Sociology of Childhood: Developmental Thinking, Categorization, and Graphic Visualization.* Cambridge: Cambridge University Press, 2008.

Turmel, André. "Das normale Kind. Zwischen Kategorisierung, Statistik und Entwicklung." In *Ganz normale Kinder. Heterogenität und Standardisierung kindlicher Entwicklung,* edited by Helga Kelle and Anja Tervooren, pp. 17–40. Weinheim: Juventa, 2008.

Ueding, Gert. "Verstoßen in ein fremdes Land. Kinderbilder der deutschen Literatur." *Neue Sammlung* 17 (1977): pp. 344–356.

Voragine, Jacobus de. *The Golden Legend: Readings on the Saints.* Translated by William Granger Ryan. Princeton: Princeton University Press, 2012.

Walser, Robert. *A Schoolboy's Diary. And Other Stories.* Translated by Damion Searls. New York: New York Review of Books, 2013.

Walser, Robert. *Aus dem Bleistiftgebiet,* edited by Bernhard Echte and Werner Morlang. 6 Volumes. Frankfurt am Main: Suhrkamp, 1985–2000.

Walser, Robert. *Briefe*, edited by Jörg Schäfer with the assistance of Robert Mächler. Frankfurt am Main: Suhrkamp, 1979.

Walser, Robert. *Masquerade and Other Stories*. Translated by Susan Bernofsky. Baltimore and London: The John Hopkins University Press, 1990.

Walser, Robert. *Microscripts*. Translated by Susan Bernofsky. New York: New Directions, 2010.

Walser, Robert. *Mikrogramme*. In *Kritische Ausgabe*, edited by Wolfram Groddeck and Barbara von Reibnitz. Basel: Schwabe/Stroemfeld, 2016–2019, sect. 6.

Walser, Robert. *Sämtliche Werke*, edited by Jochen Greven. 20 Volumes. Frankfurt am Main: Suhrkamp, 1985–1986.

Walt, Christian. *Improvisation und Interpretation. Robert Walsers Mikrogramme lesen*. Frankfurt am Main: Stroemfeld, 2015.

Walter Benjamin Archiv, ed. *Walter Benjamins Archive. Bilder, Texte und Zeichen*. Frankfurt am Main: Suhrkamp, 2006.

Weber-Kellermann, Ingeborg. *Das Weihnachtsfest. Eine Kultur- und Sozialgeschichte der Weihnachtszeit*. Luzern and Frankfurt am Main: Bucher, 1978.

Whittaker, Gwendolyn. *Überbürdung – Subversion – Ermächtigung. Die Schule und die literarische Moderne, 1880–1918*. Göttingen: V&R unipress, 2013.

Wiesbauer, Elisabeth. *Das Kind als Objekt der Wissenschaft. Medizinische und psychologische Kinderforschung an der Universität Wien, 1800–1914*. Vienna and Munich: Löcker, 1982.

Wilamowitz-Moellendorff, Ulrich von. *Euripides Herakles*. Berlin: Weidmann, 1909.

Wilhelm II. "Ansprache seiner Majestät des Kaisers und Königs." In *Verhandlungen über Fragen des höheren Unterrichts, Berlin 4. bis 17. Dezember*, pp. 70–76. Berlin: W. Hertz, 1891.

Wittmann, Barbara. "Am Anfang. Theorien des Kritzelns im 19. Jahrhundert." In *Von selbst. Autopoietische Verfahren in der Ästhetik des 19. Jahrhunderts*, edited by Friedrich Weltzien, pp. 141–154. Bonn: Reimer, 2006.

Wittmann, Barbara. *Bedeutungsvolle Kritzeleien. Eine Kultur- und Wissensgeschichte der Kinderzeichnung, 1500–1950.* Berlin and Zurich: Diaphanes, 2018.

Wittmann, Barbara. "'Drawing Cure', Die Kinderzeichnung als Instrument der Psychoanalyse." In *Spuren erzeugen. Zeichnen und Schreiben als Verfahren der Selbstaufzeichnung,* edited by Barbara Wittmann, pp. 109–144. Berlin: Diaphanes, 2009.

Wittmann, Barbara. "Zeichnen, im Dunkeln. Psychophysiologie einer Kulturtechnik um 1900." In *Randgänge der Zeichnung,* edited by Werner Busch, Oliver Jehle, and Carolin Meister, pp. 165–186. Munich: Fink, 2007.

Wohlfart, Günter. *Das spielende Kind. Nietzsche: Postvorsokratiker – Vorpostmoderner.* Essen: Die Blaue Eule, 1999.

Wulffen, Erich. *Das Kind. Sein Wesen und seine Entartung.* Berlin: Langenscheidt, 1913.

Zumbusch, Cornelia. *Die Immunität der Klassik.* Frankfurt am Main: Suhrkamp, 2011.

Zumbusch, Cornelia. "Erzählen und Erziehen. Pädagogik der Zurückhaltung in Stifters *Mappe meines Urgroßvaters.*" *Internationales Archiv für Sozialgeschichte der deutschen Literatur* 40, no. 2 (2015): pp. 479–502.

Zumbusch, Cornelia. "Nachgetragene Ursprünge. Vorgeschichten im Bildungsroman (Wieland, Goethe und Stifter)." *Poetica* 43, nos. 3–4 (2011): pp. 267–299.